Social Work
with Volunteers

Also Available from Lyceum Books, Inc.

Advisory Editors: Thomas M. Meenaghan, *New York University*
Ira Colby, *University of Houston*

NONPROFITS AND TECHNOLOGY: EMERGING RESEARCH FOR USABLE KNOWLEDGE,
by Michael Cortés and Kevin M. Rafter, foreword by Tessie Guillermo

A PRACTICAL GUIDE TO SOCIAL SERVICE EVALUATION,
by Carl F. Brun

SOCIAL WORK IN A SUSTAINABLE WORLD,
by Nancy Mary

SECONDARY TRAUMATIC STRESS AND THE CHILD WELFARE PROFESSIONAL,
by Josephine G. Pryce, Kimberly K. Shackelford, and David H. Pryce

HOW TO TEACH EFFECTIVELY,
by Bruce D. Friedman

STRAIGHT TALK ABOUT PROFESSIONAL ETHICS,
by Kim Strom-Gottfried

THE ETHICS OF PRACTICE WITH CHILDREN,
by Kim Strom-Gottfried

PRACTICAL TIPS FOR PUBLISHING SCHOLARLY ARTICLES: WRITING AND PUBLISHING IN THE HELPING PROFESSIONS,
by Rich Furman

TEAMWORK IN MULTIPROFESSIONAL CARE,
by Malcolm Payne, foreword by Thomas M. Meenaghan

ADVOCACY, ACTIVISM, AND THE INTERNET: COMMUNITY ORGANIZATION AND SOCIAL POLICY,
by Steven F. Hick and John G. McNutt

ADVOCACY PRACTICE FOR SOCIAL JUSTICE,
by Richard Hoefer

Social Work with Volunteers

Michael E. Sherr
Baylor University

LYCEUM
BOOKS, INC.

Chicago, Illinois

© Lyceum Books, Inc., 2008

Published by

LYCEUM BOOKS, INC.
5758 S. Blackstone Ave.
Chicago, Illinois 60637
773+643-1903 (Fax)
773+643-1902 (Phone)
lyceum@lyceumbooks.com
http://www.lyceumbooks.com

12 11 10 09 08   1 2 3 4 5

ISBN: 978-1-933478-11-1

Library of Congress Cataloging-in-Publication Data

Sherr, Michael E.
    Social work with volunteers / by Michael E. Sherr.
       p. cm.
    Includes bibliographical references.
    ISBN 978-1-933478-11-1 (alk. paper)
    1. Voluntarism. 2. Volunteers. I. Title.
    HN49.V64S54 2007
    361.3'7—dc22
                            2007035927

To Stacey, Brandon, Noah, and Grace
and
to Bob Wineburg—promise fulfilled

Contents

Figures and Tables

About the Author

Michael E. Sherr is assistant professor of social work in the School of Social Work at Baylor University. He is a BSSW graduate of University of North Carolina Greensboro and an MSW and PhD graduate of the College of Social Work at University of South Carolina. Professor Sherr has published extensively in social work in an eclectic array of areas including integration of faith in social work education and practice, volunteerism, end-of-life care, Afrocentrism, and rural social work. He is also assistant editor of *Social Work and Christianity*. Professor Sherr is a licensed clinical social worker and has been the director of a behavioral health clinic; as a clinician, he has worked with adults in a partial hospitalization program and children and families in a hospice setting. He is also an active volunteer for two volunteer service organizations, his church, and the community.

Foreword

Volunteers are an important part of helping efforts in the United States. They raise money, provide services, and create programs. They are the members of the boards of many human service agencies and frequently serve on commissions, panels, and other decision-making groups. They also build communities; aid victims of war, conflict, and disaster; and found new agencies. They advocate new and improved social policies. They help other nations and gain the goodwill of citizens and governments of other countries.

Volunteering has a long and proud history in organized social welfare. Research has shown that most Americans volunteer at one time or another during their lifetimes. The Corporation for National Service (2007) reports that the United States is currently experiencing almost unprecedented levels of volunteering. Organizations like the United Way, the Corporation for National Service, and the Peace Corps keep the spirit of volunteerism alive. It is this volunteer effort, in part, that builds communities and civic culture (Putnam, 2000). Historically, much of the effort to help the victims of individual and collective tragedies has come from volunteers. Even the efforts of professional helpers depend to a large extent on volunteer fundraising, advocacy, and board leadership.

Many volunteers come from religious groups. As a central tenant, most contemporary religions strongly support aiding those in need and commitment for volunteering toward that end. The role of religion and religious organizations in social welfare is both well documented and extensive. Prior to industrialization, much of the effort to help the poor was conducted by religious institutions.

The relationship between these two important forces in social welfare and the social work profession is mixed at best, and difficult in many instances. Social work has often failed to sufficiently appreciate volunteers and has, until very recently, looked askance at the contributions of many religious groups. This is clearly not a desirable situation. It is also not a sustainable situation as society evolves.

Lubove (1969) argued that in order for social work to be seen as a profession, practitioners had to distance themselves from volunteers. Their work had to be different from the types of activities that anyone could do. Otherwise, why would anyone pay social workers to do it? A similar argument was made by Specht and Courtney (1994). These beliefs have led to a disengagement from the faith community. This was not the same type of clean break (due largely to the persistence of religious agencies), but the theme of secularization has been important to the profession.

These early decisions in support of professionalization have created a strained relationship that makes it difficult for many social workers to work with volunteers or the faith community. This often runs against training, organizational culture, and practice wisdom. In the past two decades this stance has become increasingly problematic as social policy has demanded engagement with both volunteers and the faith community. This has led to tense situations and failed programs.

Michael Sherr has bravely charged into this sorry state of affairs and produced a provocative analysis of why social workers resist working with volunteers and with the faith community. He offers a strong historical analysis and suggests that social work should move beyond its early beliefs and assumptions concerning volunteers and the faith community.

To that end, Sherr offers social workers conceptual tools to integrate these two often overlapping groups into their practice. His work carefully delineates the issues that divide the social work profession from the volunteer and faith communities.

In addition to the analysis of the issues involved in collaboration, he outlines the skills practitioners must acquire to work successfully with volunteers. These include recruiting volunteers, developing and managing programs, and other facets of the volunteer administration process. The material is intelligent and based in current literature from multiple fields.

Sherr is very careful to combine material about volunteer administration, communities of faith, and social work theory into a coherent and understandable whole. This makes the book easy to incorporate into traditional social work courses because the familiar content acts as a bridge between the new material in the book and what already exists in the curriculum.

This is a useful and thought-provoking book. It should be read by anyone with an interest in the future of social work.

John G. McNutt, PhD
Professor
School of Urban Affairs and Public Policy
Center for Community Research and Service
University of Delaware

References

Corporation for National Service. (2007, July). *Issue brief: Volunteering in America—an overview of corporation research.* Retrieved September 20, 2007, from http://www.nationalservice.org/pdf/07_0712_via_issuebrief.pdf

Lubove, R. (1969). *The professional altruist: The emergence of social work as a career, 1880–1930.* New York: Macmillan.

Putnam, R. D. (2000). *Bowling alone: The collapse and revival of American community.* New York: Touchstone.

Specht, H., & Courtney, M. E. (1994). *Unfaithful angels: How social work has abandoned its mission.* New York: Free Press.

Preface

The landscape of social welfare services has shifted over the past two decades, creating unique opportunities and challenges for communities, organizations, and the profession of social work. The provision of services is no longer the primary responsibility of the federal government and is becoming the shared responsibility of public, private, and nonprofit organizations at the state and local levels. Along with this shift, there has been a concerted effort to encourage more volunteers to participate in addressing social concerns. As the primary profession in the development, provision, and evaluation of social services, social workers are in a position to shape how agency administrators, direct staff, and volunteers work together to provide services. The purpose of this book is to offer a new way of thinking about social work practice with volunteers and set forth the context-specific optimal partnership model to assist readers to create effective partnerships.

A major theme of the book is that volunteerism is a complex phenomenon. Social workers who want to effectively organize, partner, or lead volunteer activities must first become familiar with the complex nature of volunteerism. Volunteering is significantly different from other helping behaviors. Volunteers seek out opportunities to help, rather than reacting to situations that confront them. They consciously decide whether or not to join a group of others who volunteer, how deeply to get involved, and how much each volunteer opportunity fits into their lives. People are motivated to volunteer for many different reasons including, for example, religion, politics, personal development, and self-esteem enhancement. As people continue to volunteer, their goals may or may not be met, and their motivations may become quite different over time.

Part I examines the nature of volunteerism. The first chapter establishes a comprehensive definition for volunteerism. After highlighting the debate in the literature over what constitutes volunteering, I provide a comprehensive definition with four distinct elements that will serve as a foundation for the rest of the book. The second chapter describes all the reasons why people volunteer. Recruiting and retaining a dedicated cadre of volunteers is the cornerstone of any partnership between social workers and volunteers. Chapter 2 is meant to provide social workers with a detailed description of the major reasons people decide to volunteer and the reasons they decide to continue.

In chapter 3 a human behavior theoretical framework for describing social work with volunteers is explored. A critical analysis of volunteerism with relevant HBSE theories is consistent with the strengths perspective common to social work.

Volunteerism is a phenomenon that encourages capacity building while simultaneously addressing social problems. When social workers view individuals, families, and communities as potential volunteer partners in providing services, reciprocal relationships that enhance the dignity and worth of all people, especially vulnerable populations, are promoted.

The focus of this volume is on *reframing* the current shift in American social welfare in the context of the historical relationship between volunteerism and social work. A primary thesis of the book is that the current shift in social welfare is most accurately described as progress forward rather than devolution, a perspective so pervasive in the social work profession. Volunteerism preceded social work in almost every field of practice. In fact, social work owes its existence to volunteerism. How did social work, which owes its existence to volunteerism, lose touch with volunteerism as a central means of delivering effective services and advocating for social and economic justice? An historical review of the relationship between volunteerism and social work is necessary in order to understand what occurred and reframe how the current shift is perceived.

Part II reviews the historical relationship between social work and volunteerism. Chapter 4 describes Jane Addams's work as a social worker and volunteer. A detailed look at the literature written by and about Jane Addams reveals a pattern in her approach to social work practice. The foundation of all her accomplishments was her belief in the usefulness of volunteers and her ability to recognize, develop, and embrace the volunteer motivations of all people. Chapter 5 examines the transition away from how Jane Addams and other prominent social work pioneers practiced social work to where social work practice is today. The chapter describes three discernable periods in the relationship between social work and volunteerism and concludes with a discussion of some reasons for the transition.

In chapter 6, special attention is given to the impact of religion on social work with volunteers. A major premise of this book is that one cannot adequately address the relationship between social work and volunteerism without taking into account the influence of religion. After reviewing the religious foundations for volunteer service in several world religions, the chapter examines the role that religious groups play in promoting volunteerism and the extent of volunteer contributions made by religious groups. The chapter concludes with a discussion of social work's skittishness with religion and how that has affected its relationship with volunteers. Similarities between the motives of the social work profession and religiously motivated volunteers are highlighted as a way of encouraging social workers to build partnerships based on common ground.

Part III introduces the context-specific optimal partnership (CSOP) model as a new approach to working with volunteers. In chapter 7, the CSOP model is put forth as the next progressive step in how social welfare policy and programs work in this country. Instead of predetermining the roles of the public, private, professional, religious, and volunteer sectors, the CSOP model calls for the unique circumstances of each social problem to determine what roles each sector will play in developing and delivering social welfare services. In chapter 8, the CSOP model is put into action. In-depth case examples using the CSOP model emphasize how each unique scenario calls for different formulas for achieving optimal partnerships between social workers and volunteers. Chapter 9 provides social workers with resources for finding volunteers for partnerships. The chapter begins with a discussion of strategies to help social workers find volunteers for partnerships in any community. A reference list of many of the major volunteer organizations, each with a brief description and contact information, is intended to serve as a starting point for social workers to develop partnerships with volunteers. Finally, chapter 10 examines community and organization parameters that influence social work practice with volunteers. The chapter concludes by providing social workers with specific strategies for changing the context of optimal partnerships.

As the first book to specifically address social work with volunteers, this book is intended for two audiences. First of all, the book is meant to assist practitioners as the decrease in government support means that more and more volunteers are needed to assist in delivering services. By reframing the current shift in social welfare and learning to use the CSOP model, social work practitioners will be more effective in carrying out the mission of the profession—"to enhance human well-being and help meet the basic human needs of all people, with particular attention to the needs and empowerment of people who are vulnerable, oppressed, and living in poverty" (National Association of Social Workers, 1999).

The book is also intended for use in social work practice courses on working with communities and organizations. Although macropractice texts provide students with ample content to understand social problems, analyze communities, and work within organizations, volunteerism as a complex social and behavioral phenomenon is not adequately addressed (see, e.g., Brueggemann, 2002; Fellin, 2001; Kirst-Ashman & Hull, 2006; Rothman, Erlich, & Tropman, 2001). Nevertheless, the ability to recruit and retain committed volunteers is often the key factor affecting the usefulness and stability of any grassroots movement, community coalition, or innovative organizational planning. Given the complex nature of volunteerism and the expanding role that volunteerism will play in future social welfare services, the topic warrants comprehensive coverage to prepare students for competent practice.

Acknowledgments

There are so many people whose friendship, love, and support have helped make this work possible. First is my family. Without Stacey, my wife and partner for the last seventeen years, I would never have had the courage and persistence to write this book. My children, Brandon, Noah, and Grace, kept me grounded during my research and long hours of writing. While writing, I often thought of my children, wanting them to grow up to be giving and caring people who make volunteering and service to others an essential part of their life journeys. I also say thanks to my father and Uncle Jay for being living examples of unconditional love, forgiveness, and support.

Terry Wolfer, my mentor, friend, and staunch supporter, deserves a lot of credit for this work. When I shared with him a rough outline for what would become the underlying framework of this book, he listened, encouraged me, and helped mold my thinking and approach to what I wanted to say about social work with volunteers. I also owe a debt of gratitude to Naomi Farber, Miriam Johnson, and Andrew Billingsley for their support and feedback on early drafts of this work. I need to thank Leon Ginsberg and the rest of the faculty at the College of Social Work at the University of South Carolina. What a welcoming, challenging, and loving environment for doctoral studies.

To Bob Wineburg, Jefferson Pilot Excellence Professor in the Department of Social Work at the University of North Carolina Greensboro, whose book, *A Limited Partnership,* inspired this book, I say thanks. I consider it a great privilege to be one of his students. Although he knows that we see things differently, as my teacher and now my colleague, he has been supportive from day one.

The last few people I want to thank on the scholarship side of things are Carolyn Lancaster, David Follmer, and Tom Meenaghan. This book would simply not exist without the patience and careful editorial eye of Carolyn Lancaster. She was patient and gentle in her critiques, making sure that what I had to say sounded good to others, not just me. Thanks, Carolyn! To David and Tom, thank you for your support, caring, and firm critiques, but most of all, your belief in me. David, I am so grateful to you for making me feel part of the Lyceum family. Finally, to those mentors, friends, students, and colleagues I have not mentioned, thank you.

Part I

Volunteerism: A Complex Phenomenon

1

Defining Volunteerism

AT AGE THIRTY-FIVE, DARYL REYNOLDS HAS A VERY FULL LIFE. HE HAS BEEN married to his wife, Tracy, for twelve years, and they have two children: Thomas, age seven, and Kinsey, age four. Daryl lives in Oregon, where he is a computer engineer for a high-tech company that makes computers and disc drives for backing up storage files. On a typical day, Daryl leaves for work around 7:30 and arrives home around 6:00. On Tuesdays Daryl and Tracy take Thomas to basketball practice, and on Mondays Kinsey has soccer practice. On Wednesday evenings Daryl stays home alone with the children while Tracy goes out with several of her friends for their weekly girls' night out. On top of everything else, Daryl also tutors children in math every Thursday evening at the Jackson County Boys and Girls Club.

Daryl began tutoring children sixteen years ago in college as part of an assignment for a service learning elective he completed during his sophomore year. During the semester, he was required to volunteer for forty hours and write a reflection paper at the end of his experience. At first he did not know where he should volunteer. He did know, however, that he wanted to find something simple and short term to do to complete the assignment. He had no intention of continuing to volunteer once the course was over. At the dining commons he saw a flier advertising for students to provide tutoring for children in an after-school program sponsored by the Boys and Girls Club. He called the number and scheduled an appointment to meet with the program director the next day. At the meeting, the program director handed Daryl a schedule for the after-school program and asked him to identify his strongest subject and three times during the week when he could come to the program. Daryl shared that he loves math and would be willing to tutor children for an hour on Mondays, Tuesdays, and Thursdays until the end of his semester. He has been tutoring children in math ever since.

Since college, Daryl's responsibilities shifted as he married, started a family, and became a computer engineer. He simply did not have the amount of time necessary to continue tutoring at the Boys and Girls Club three nights a week. However, working with the children had become important to him. He enjoyed watching the children develop a sense of mastery with math. He also felt that tutoring children helped him to maintain his love for math, especially when he was feeling stressed about things at work. He and Tracy decided that he could volunteer at the Boys and Girls Club one night a week.

On occasion, Daryl also takes on other volunteer activities at the Boys and Girls Club. Each year at Thanksgiving, Daryl and his entire family work in the kitchen at the club, preparing Thanksgiving meals for hundreds of children. Thomas and Kinsey even help organize silverware, fold napkins, and decorate the dining area. Four years ago Daryl spearheaded a fund-raising venture between his company, the club, and the community to build a computer lab for the after-school program. The owners of his company agreed to sell the club computer equipment for the lab at cost. Meanwhile, Daryl and the program director would organize several fund-raising events to allow the club to purchase the computers. It took eight months to raise enough money to purchase the computers. During that time, in addition to tutoring on Thursdays, Daryl spent three hours each Saturday morning helping to organize and participate in fund-raisers.

It's been four years since Estella Gomez's husband died from cancer. Estella and Manuel were happily married for thirty-two years. Manuel was a successful real estate investor and Estella stayed home to raise their daughter, Sonya. After Sonya left for college, Estella and Manuel really enjoyed taking long vacations to see their family in Mexico. During their last trip, Estella noticed that Manuel was forgetting things she had just said to him, and she scheduled an appointment for him to see the doctor. After the doctor referred them to a neurologist, they discovered that Manuel had an inoperable brain tumor. Manuel died three months later, two days before his fifty-eighth birthday. During the three months before he died, Manuel received palliative care services from Mountain Valley Hospice. Although Estella cared for Manuel's day-to-day needs, a nurse visited each week to make sure his pain was manageable, and a hospice volunteer came to spend time with Manuel so Estella could get out of the house to run errands. After Manuel died, the hospice provided Estella with bereavement services, including an eight-week grief support group for spouses. A licensed clinical social worker facilitated the support group.

By the time the support group came to an end, Estella had developed a close friendship with Melissa, a group member whose husband died of a heart attack a few weeks before Manuel died. Over the next year, Melissa and Estella spent time doing things together for companionship. They would go shopping, eat meals together, and play cards on Saturdays at the local country club. Eventually Melissa invited Estella to join her at St. Martin's Cathedral for church on Sundays. One Sunday, the priest invited a man from Mountain Valley Hospice to set up a display and talk with congregants about volunteering with hospice. Estella and Melissa decided to sign up to volunteer together.

At first, Estella and Melissa attended a series of training workshops to learn about the history of hospice care, the history of Mountain Valley Hospice, and the roles volunteers play in delivering palliative care. As a last step before volunteer-

ing, they had to present proof that their immunizations were up to date. Melissa moved back home to get married to her high school sweetheart shortly after finishing the training. She was never assigned a family and has not volunteered anywhere since then.

Estella decided she wanted to provide companionship care for patients and their families. She was assigned to different families each week. On Mondays, Wednesdays, and Fridays, she would spend three hours in the afternoons providing respite care, transporting patients to and from doctor's appointments, and cleaning and cooking for family members. In the two years since she began volunteering, Estella has worked with twelve different families. Last month Estella completed a fourteen-hour training curriculum to become a hospice 101 volunteer. As a hospice 101 volunteer, Estella makes presentations once a month to local businesses, civic clubs, nursing homes, and churches, telling people about hospice and helping recruit more volunteers. The only payment Estella receives is reimbursement for her mileage whenever she drives to patients' homes, transports patients to appointments, and travels to speak with people in the community.

At age twenty-five, Aaron is in his second year of working for Southland Mortgage as a loan officer. When he was hired, he knew that the owner of Southland Mortgage required all his loan officers to get involved in some type of volunteer service association. He even paid the membership dues for his loan officers to join. The owner thought it was important for loan officers to develop good social networks and good public relations with potential customers in the community. As time went on, however, Aaron never seemed to find the time to get involved. Finally, one morning the owner called Aaron into his office and told him that he was going to be a colleague's guest at the Lions Club meeting at noon the next day. Aaron tried to come up with a reason why he couldn't go but ultimately agreed, as the owner insisted.

Late the next morning Aaron went with Jason to the Lions Club meeting that met each week in the back room of the Hong Kong Restaurant. As they arrived at the meeting, he noticed Jason put on a yellow vest that had a number of pins on it and the Lions Club insignia on the back. After they found their seats in the back room, Jason told Aaron to go get his lunch from the buffet because the meeting was about to start. A minute later Aaron heard a lion's roar coming from the thirty-two people in the back room and wondered if this kind of club was for him.

During the meeting, Jason introduced Aaron to several different people. Aaron met an accountant from a competing bank, a funeral director, a school teacher, an insurance broker, the chief of police, an eye doctor, and a college professor. He also met Robert, the president of the club, who welcomed him and gave him a brochure about the Lions. Robert also invited Aaron to attend the club's annual chili cook-off on Saturday to raise money to purchase eyeglasses for people who could not afford them. Robert explained that the club was still short one person to sell tickets at the booth between 2:00 and 4:00 in the afternoon. Aaron accepted the invitation.

That Saturday Aaron ended up helping all afternoon. In addition to working the ticket booth, he wound up serving chili, clearing off tables, and counting the proceeds at the end of the event. At the next meeting, he filled out his application, paid his dues (for which he would be reimbursed by the owner of his company), and became an official member of the Lions Club.

Over the next year, Robert continued asking Aaron to help with different community service projects. Aaron handed out candy at a local Wal-Mart, sold tree ornaments in the mall before Christmas, and worked with the entire club to build a house with Habitat for Humanity. Aaron also developed a number of friendships from the club, and a few members even referred people who were looking for a loan to him. At the last meeting, Aaron was elected treasurer, and next year he plans to attend the Lions International Convention in Osaka, Japan. He plans to pay his own expenses.

Daryl Reynolds, Estella Gomez, and Aaron Freeman are three people with completely different life stories. Each of them has experienced different life circumstances, has different interests and different strengths, and is at a different point in his or her life course. In the same way, each of them had different reasons for becoming a volunteer. For Daryl, becoming a volunteer began simply as a way of completing a class assignment. For Estella, after months of grieving and developing new supports, a chance encounter at a church, along with the encouragement of a friend, motivated her to take the initiative to become a hospice volunteer. Aaron was somewhat coerced into attending a meeting at a volunteer association. Attending and becoming a member of the Lions began simply as a part of his job. In addition, they volunteer in a variety of ways. Daryl works with children, Estella primarily works with people facing a terminal illness, and Aaron works with people in the community, doing all sorts of different community activities. What is it about what they are doing that makes them volunteers? Moreover, what are some of the reasons that each of them continues to volunteer? How did Daryl and Aaron go from not being fully involved to becoming committed volunteers? Why did Estella remain a volunteer while her friend Melissa never volunteered after finishing her training?

The questions that arise from these three vignettes demonstrate the challenges of understanding volunteerism. As in the vignettes, people have different experiences, unique life courses, and various strengths. Understanding how people become and remain volunteers requires knowing and appreciating all the systems that affect their lives. For social workers, understanding begins with appreciating volunteerism as a complex area of practice that is essential to working effectively with communities and organizations.

This chapter sets forth a working definition of volunteerism that will serve as the foundation for the rest of the book. The chapter will also define volunteer association, volunteer membership, and volunteer commitment—three concepts with which one must be familiar in order to develop a comprehensive understanding of volunteerism. The three vignettes will serve to illustrate the concepts throughout the chapter.

WHAT IS VOLUNTEERISM?

The definition of volunteerism may seem self-evident. The literature, however, does not offer a consensus on a single definition. Rather there are different perspectives describing volunteerism as any work without pay, a complex phenomenon, and helping behavior that is somehow connected to religious practices or beliefs.

Work without Pay

Studies on volunteerism started off as an extension of the business and psychology literature attempting to understand work (Brayfield & Rothe, 1951; Herzberg, Mausner, & Snyderman, 1959; Vroom, 1964). The studies tended to compare and contrast the motivations and satisfactions of volunteerism (work without pay) with the motivations and satisfactions of paid work (Naylor, 1967; Pearce, 1983; Sills, 1957). The influence of this view was evident in Gidron's (1985) comparison of the similarities and differences between the two. He described both volunteerism and work as "involving a situation where there is a job to be done," and "work [that] is performed within a specific organizational context, under specific conditions, which could be rewarding or stressful, with set relationships to supervisors, peers and sometimes subordinates" (p. 3). He described payment as the main difference: "The pay element in paid work represents, among other things, the necessity to work, the fact that one has to work in order to survive economically. This means a different form of relationship to the place of work, a different form of compliance. The level of pay is a form of recognition. In many cases, volunteer work is an addition to and not a substitute for the major activity in which one is paid for work" (p. 4). Since then, distinct lines of research with elaborate methodologies have attempted to predict and measure motivations for and satisfactions of volunteerism (e.g., Cnaan & Goldberg-Glen, 1991; Field & Johnson, 1993; Galindo-Kuhn & Guzley, 2001). Nevertheless, the underlying perspective of each line of inquiry reduces the definition of volunteerism to work without pay. The three vignettes will demonstrate the problems with this basic view.

At first glance, Daryl, Estella, and Aaron all appear engaged in activities where they provide work without pay. A closer look at what each of them was doing, however, reveals that their activities cannot be explained by this basic view. Daryl's activities with the Boys and Girls Club appear to come closest to fitting the definition of providing work without pay. His primary activity was providing an hour of math tutoring each week without pay. But what about the time he helped organize fund-raising with his company and the agency? He must have spent time working with people at the company and talking about the computer lab. For at least some of that time, he was probably being paid while he was at work. Technically, he was being paid for some portion of his activity.

Before Estella began working with families, she had to complete a series of workshops and make sure her immunizations were up to date. During that time, Estella was not providing services; she was receiving training. In the same way, her friend Melissa never provided services; her involvement with volunteering was limited to the training she received. In addition, Estella received mileage reimbursement whenever she traveled to see families, transported patients to and from appointments, and went to speak with people in the community. Although the amount of reimbursement may be small, she did receive some form of payment for her work.

As a Lion, Aaron was not a volunteer when he went to his first meeting. He (actually his boss) paid dues so that he could spend most of his time eating lunch, networking with others, and talking about providing services. Then, on occasion, he chose to spend additional time participating in community service projects. It would have been quite possible for Aaron just to pay membership dues, attend the weekly meetings, and never participate in the service projects. Moreover, in some volunteer organizations, all Aaron would have to do is pay his membership dues—he wouldn't even have to attend meetings. His activity would certainly not be considered work—with or without pay.

A Complex Phenomenon

Instead of describing volunteerism as work without pay, some scholars view volunteerism as a phenomenon that is influenced by a number of individual and environmental factors (e.g., Sherr, 2003a, 2003b; Wilson & Musick, 1997). Paolicchi (1995) suggests that volunteerism is a complex construct that cannot be defined by a single characteristic (e.g., work without pay). He suggests that studies building upon a single trait or activity distort the nature of volunteerism because they presume to search for universal and formal laws of behavior. Volunteers are people of all ages and are intrinsically motivated by physiological, cognitive, and emotional reasons influenced by a host of external factors such as family and social networks, education, socioeconomic status, religious or spiritual teachings, political leanings, and the degree to which their culture emphasizes the importance of social concern and helping others. There is also a great deal of individual-to-individual variability as to which factors are important in influencing a person to volunteer. Furthermore, the reasons and influences leading people to become volunteers can change as they have new experiences, so that in time the reasons they continue volunteering could be very different from the reasons they started. Given this view, it becomes important to understand volunteerism as an activity that occurs due to an interplay of factors within the unique life experiences of individuals.

Another way of describing the complex nature of volunteerism is as an activity brought about by the interplay of different types of capital. Coleman (1994) defines capital as "a resource or factor input that facilitates production, but is not consumed or otherwise used up in production" (p. 175). In the context of volunteerism, three types of capital can interact to bring about the likelihood that someone will engage in volunteer activity. Human capital refers to the individual resources, including health status, education, and income, that make volunteerism possible. Social capital refers to all the social connections that may make someone more likely to volunteer. Cultural capital consists of learned attitudes, knowledge, and preferences that prepare people to volunteer. In general, a certain mixture of the three types of capital makes an individual likely to volunteer (Wilson & Musick, 1997).

In the context of social work, volunteerism should be thought of as preceding the profession in almost every field of practice (Anderson & Ambrosino, 1992). In the seventeenth century, groups of volunteers worked together to create benevolent societies to provide relief to the poor when their families could not (Fairlie, 1920). In the eighteenth and nineteenth centuries, the efforts of volunteers improved transportation, sanitation, communication, fire prevention, public safety, and education. Volunteers also advocated fair labor practices, women's rights, African Americans' rights, better medical practices, and humane treatment for the mentally ill. Even the social reform advances of the Progressive Era depended upon volunteers working to get the government directly involved in social welfare (Hofstadter, 1963). Most notably, the contributions of volunteers were essential to the development of the Charity Organization Society movement and the settlement house movement—both of which were linked to the emergence of the social work profession.

In terms of practice with individuals, groups, and communities, a few other descriptions of volunteerism are especially pertinent for social workers to consider. First, volunteerism is one of the few activities that can simultaneously enhance client well-being while offering the opportunity to promote social reform or address a social problem (Sherr, 2003b). In direct practice, encouraging clients to get involved in volunteerism can help reduce psychological distress; improve view of self; promote feelings of acceptance, purpose, and belonging; increase opportunities for positive social interaction, and improve overall life satisfaction (Black & DiNitto, 1994; Morrow-Howell, Kinnevy, & Mann, 1999; Rietschlin, 1998). At the same time, clients who begin volunteering are more likely to get involved in other community affairs and recruit others to volunteer (Danoff & Kopel, 1994; Stevens, 1991; Stukas, Snyder, & Clary, 1999). Second, volunteerism promotes reciprocal relationships—a hallmark of the social work helping process. In client-helper relationships, whether intended or not, social workers are in a position of power and authority as the people providing help to clients who receive help. For example, when a social worker provides counseling to a family with a child who has autism, the social worker is ultimately deemed the professional by society, while the family is deemed the client. When the social worker and the family volunteer for an association raising awareness of the needs of children with autism, however, they are both concerned citizens addressing a social problem. Furthermore, new policies, programs, resources, and funds developed as a result of volunteering may ultimately help the social worker to assist clients in the future. Lastly, from a strengths perspective, volunteerism is one of the few activities that practitioners can analyze with relevant social work theories without focusing on pathology or deficits.

In the context of this broader view of volunteerism as a complex phenomenon, the experiences of Daryl, Estella, and Aaron can be understood in terms of interactions between person-in-environment factors. For Daryl, a course assignment (an environmental factor) prompted him to begin volunteering. His initial motivation interacted with his aptitude for math and his internal desire to complete the course (personal factors) to guide him to call the Boys and Girls Club. In the same way, Aaron began volunteering only after the owner of his company insisted he attend a meeting (environmental factor). The owner's insistence was strong enough to overcome Aaron's initial discomfort. As he accepted invitations to participate in community service projects, he eventually became comfortable, made friends with others, and became an active volunteer. It was his educational training (personal factor), however, that allowed him to work as a loan officer for a company that required and paid for him to become a volunteer. Estella's grief (personal factors) over the death of her husband (environmental factor) led to her participation in a support group sponsored by the hospice. During the support group, she developed a friendship with Melissa that eventually resulted in her becoming a hospice volunteer (environmental factors). She went from being the client receiving services to a volunteer working side by side with the people who had assisted her and her husband—a true example of a reciprocal and empowering helping relationship.

A Helping Behavior Connected to Religious Practices or Beliefs

The impact of religion on volunteerism is the focus of chapter 6. For present purposes, a few general comments are sufficient. First, religious beliefs and practices are one way that values are defined in societies. According to Parsons (1977), in addition to empirical knowledge, religious beliefs and practices establish and reinforce values that create commitment to a social system. There is enough evidence to support the claim that religious beliefs and practices play an important role in understanding volunteerism, especially in America (Curtis, Grabb, & Baer, 1992; Greeley, 1997; Wuthnow, 2004). There are competing theories explaining the relationship between religion and volunteerism. For example, volunteerism is seen by some as a direct expression of religious beliefs (e.g., Ammerman, 2001; Billingsley, 1999; Sider, Olson, & Unruh, 2002). Others believe that Religious beliefs and practices encourage group norms that foster cultures of volunteerism (Cnaan, Kasternakis, & Wineburg, 1993; Wilson & Janoski, 1995). Regardless of the reasons behind the relationship between religion and volunteerism, recognizing and appreciating the link between volunteerism and religion is a key for effective social work practice with volunteers (Sherr & Shields, 2005; Sherr & Straughan, 2005).

A WORKING DEFINITION OF VOLUNTEERISM

A summary of the previous section demonstrates the difficulty of setting forth an adequate definition of volunteerism. In many cases, volunteerism involves some type of service or work without pay. On its own, however, work without pay does not account for all the variability involved when people volunteer. Approaching volunteerism as a complex phenomenon allows us to take into account all the potential interacting factors. Still, there must be something similar about what Daryl, Estella, and Aaron were doing that makes them volunteers. In addition, any definition we settle on must allow for the likelihood that religious practices and beliefs play an important role in volunteering.

With these viewpoints in mind, volunteerism is defined in this book as making a choice to act in recognition of a need, with an attitude of social responsibility and without concern for monetary profit. The choice to act must be considered to go beyond one's basic obligations (Ellis & Noyes, 1990). This definition is more comprehensive than viewing volunteering merely as unpaid labor, yet general enough to allow us to examine why people volunteer (e.g., religion) and the different degrees of volunteer participation. This definition consists of four distinct elements that warrant elaboration.

Volunteerism Is a Choice

Volunteerism involves free will or choice. People can choose to volunteer simply because they want to do so. What this means is that volunteering, in the truest sense of the word, is not forced work for any reason. Volunteering is one choice people can make about how to spend their free time. Given that volunteers often address the plights of our society (e.g., homelessness, crime prevention, HIV/AIDS, child abuse, environmental hazards), volunteering is not something usually entered into on a whim but with consideration. In contrast, getting a paying job or deciding to go to college are not completely acts of volition, but subtly coercive in origin. People go to college and enter work because they need to earn money and because society looks down on those who are able bodied and do not work.

Daryl, Estella, and Aaron all chose to volunteer. Estella and her friend Melissa chose to sign up for the training to become hospice volunteers. Eventually Estella chose to become involved as a hospice volunteer and Melissa did not. Although Daryl did not begin volunteering completely by free will, he did choose to continue after he had completed the assignment. All Aaron had to do was go to a weekly meeting and eat lunch. He made a choice to get more involved. Daryl and Aaron are also good examples of how some people begin participating in activities without technically being volunteers only to later become volunteers. This transition is an important consideration in social work practice with volunteers and will be explored further in the next chapter.

Volunteerism Involves an Attitude of Social Responsibility

Next, volunteerism involves an attitude of social responsibility. While the individuals volunteering may benefit from their activity, the explicit purpose of volunteering is to benefit others. Ellis and Noyes (1990) compare the work of graffiti artists and civil rights activists. Even though both types of work may involve a choice, only civil rights activists are motivated by their desire to work for the common good and improve society. The fact that volunteerism involves an attitude of social responsibility, however, does not mean that there are "right" and "wrong" volunteer efforts. People volunteering can support opposing sides of an issue and still be thought of as working for the common good.

The current debate over illegal immigration in the United States serves as a good example. A person may believe that immigration laws need to be reformed to make it easier for people to become legal citizens. He might give some of his time and resources by participating with a grassroots organization to educate the public about the need for reform. Another person may believe that the borders of the country should be more secure, making it more difficult for illegal immigration to occur. She might spend some of her time becoming a reserve officer assisting police officers to secure the borders of her community. Although they have completely different views and concerns about illegal immigration, they should both be considered volunteers working for the common good because "It does not matter which side is right, just that each believes its actions are socially responsible" (Ellis & Noyes, 1990, p. 3).

Volunteerism Involves a Lack of Concern for Monetary Profit

People who volunteer are not concerned about monetary profit. A lack of concern for monetary profit, however, must be distinguished from working without pay. As described earlier, some scholars view volunteerism and payment as mutually exclusive—employment is paid; volunteering is not paid (Gidron,1983; Scheier, 1980; Stebbins, 1996). Other scholars classify volunteer work in categories according to the amount of monetary payment (Clary, Snyder, & Ridge, 1992; Galindo-Kuhn & Guzley, 2001; Thompson, 1995). Smith (1981) posits that the degree to which one is a volunteer can be classified according to the amount of payment received for the value of the service. He provides three examples: "A low skilled Peace

Corps Volunteer receiving both expenses and a stipend may indeed not be a volunteer at all, but merely a low paid worker. In contrast, a law school professor who forgoes private practice, either totally or partially, because of dedication to teaching and research on the law may be viewed as a quasi-volunteer, assuming an average academic salary. Pure volunteers, in the sense of people fitting the ideal type construct best, would be individuals receiving no remuneration whatsoever while performing very valuable services" (p. 23). This definition is a compromise. It is broad enough to include volunteers who are remunerated for expenses necessary to complete work assignments (e.g., paying for needed equipment and for traveling expenses such as airfare, mileage, food, and lodging), though it clearly excludes payment that is meant as a salary in exchange for services. This broader view can now account for some of the particularities described in the cases of Daryl, Estella, and Aaron. Moreover, the definition allows for consideration of other types of personal gains, including intrapersonal and interpersonal growth, leadership training, career growth and exploration, improved social status, academic credit, and even potential for eventual employment.

Volunteerism Requires Going Beyond Basic Obligations

Saying that volunteering is a choice to act beyond basic obligations means that in many cases volunteerism is in addition to, not a substitute for, what is generally expected. Stated differently, volunteerism is different from more informal episodic acts of helping. Volunteerism occurs when people consciously seek out opportunities to help. It usually involves formally deciding to join an organization with others who volunteer, as well as how deeply to get involved, how volunteering may fit in with the rest of one's life, and if and when it is time to begin doing something different. In contrast, informal episodic acts tend to happen when people are confronted with spontaneous opportunities to help others. Some examples are helping a neighbor carry in groceries and searching a parking lot to help a stranger find his or her car. In each of the examples, an unexpected situation created an opportunity for immediate action. Ellis and Noyes (1990) point out that other helpful actions, including voting, recycling, and providing care to a family member suffering from an illness, are outside the scope of volunteerism. Instead, they are generally perceived as basic responsibilities. In each of their situations, Daryl, Estella, and Aaron participated in helping activities that are beyond their basic obligations.

ADDITIONAL CONCEPTS RELATED TO VOLUNTEERISM

Three additional concepts play an important role in effective social work practice with volunteers.

Volunteer Associations

As an extension of the definition of volunteering, volunteer associations are membership groups developed by and comprised of volunteers (Ellis & Noyes,

1990). Although volunteer associations can embrace a vast collection of purposes, structures, and operational procedures, all volunteer associations share some basic common features. For instance, almost all volunteer associations are formally constituted, organizationally separate from government, nonprofit, self-governing, and voluntary to a significant degree (Salamon & Anheier, 1996). Under this definition, volunteer associations can range from environmental groups and civic service groups to religious congregations. They can also include volunteer departments in hospitals, in social service agencies, and in Parent Teacher Associations.

Volunteer associations serve an important role in social welfare services and in the overall structure in a functioning democracy (McLean, Shultz, & Steger, 2002). For social welfare, volunteer associations offer an abundance of untapped resources for developing, implementing, and shoring up areas of needed services. Within these associations are the pastors, bankers, social workers, political leaders, business owners, doctors, and lawyers of the community. There are also the farmers, factory workers, homemakers; the unemployed; the physically and mentally challenged; the formally educated; and high school dropouts. In terms of maintaining a functioning democracy, volunteer associations represent one of the primary mediating structures between individuals and large institutions (Berger & Neuhaus, 1977). Volunteer associations encourage individual expression of values in a way that will be heard while also being socially acceptable. They also provide a buffer for stability between the government and individuals. Furthermore, by providing structures for individuals to interact and work together toward public purposes, volunteer associations are a repository for the human capital, social capital, and cultural capital needed to encourage more volunteerism (Putnam, 2000).

Although not widely discussed as part of social work education and practice, a few scholars have recognized the significance of volunteer associations. Brueggemann (2002) suggests volunteer associations are usually different from large public social service organizations because they more closely reflect the values and concerns of community members. Theilen and Poole (1986) assert that volunteer associations are one of the most effective, yet overlooked, avenues that social workers have to achieve social change. They recommend that social workers interested in social change consider "forming, holding membership in, or collaborating with volunteer associations" (p. 20), an important part of professional practice.

Volunteer Membership

Volunteer membership means affiliation with a volunteer group or organization. Membership can be formal or informal, and members' degree of involvement can vary. Participation among members can range from being a name on a volunteer list or roster, paying dues, attending meetings, providing helpful services, working on time-limited projects, helping with ongoing projects, coordinating projects, or serving on committees to holding a leadership position (Ellis & Noyes,

1990). It is important to note that members of a volunteer association (for example, those for whom union membership is mandatory or who are assigned by an employer) may not automatically be considered volunteers. Once members choose to begin participating or assuming more active roles, then they are considered volunteers. Therefore, participation in volunteer associations can range from voluntary activity to involuntary membership.

Volunteer Commitment

Volunteer commitment is the most critical concept for social work practice with volunteers (Sherr, 2003b). In working with volunteers to develop and implement service programs, social workers need to know who will volunteer, how much time they will devote, and how long they will participate in the program. The standard definition of commitment used in research on volunteerism, however, is not sufficient. Until recently, volunteer commitment was conceptualized in research as a person's intent to continue volunteering for one year from the time of a study (e.g., Clary et al., 1996). While assessing individuals' intentions to continue volunteering is certainly important, on its own, it does not offer social workers any real guidance as to how much they can count on the participation of volunteers. Therefore, what is needed is a new way of conceptualizing commitment that provides for greater detail and distinction. To this end, several scholars have suggested strengthening the definition of commitment to encompass multiple items (Clary et al., 1996; Galindo-Kuhn & Guzley, 2001).

In her research on the successes and failures of communes, Kanter (1972) found that the difference between the success and failure of a group lies in how strongly members of the group build commitment. To Kanter, commitment is much more than intending to stay. It is a connection between self-interest and group interest where, to a great extent, the group gets what it needs to maintain the community while individuals get what they need from the group to nourish their sense of self-identity. Commitment "reflects how members become committed to the community's work, to its values, and to each other, and to how much of their former independence they are willing to suspend in the interests of the group. Committed members work hard, participate actively, derive love and affection from the communal group, and believe strongly in what the group stands for" (Kanter, 1972, p. 65). Kanter's work has been incorporated to formulate the concept of "active and sustained commitment" (Sherr, 2003b, p. 25). Active and sustained commitment is defined as a construct consisting of several factors:

- ◆ The internal degree to which individuals identify themselves as volunteers
- ◆ The degree to which individuals take on or intend to take on leadership roles as volunteers
- ◆ The actual number of times people volunteered during the previous year
- ◆ The amount of time people spend volunteering each time they volunteer

- ◆ The total duration of time people have been volunteering
- ◆ Volunteers' intent to continue volunteering
- ◆ The different types of volunteer experiences (Sherr, 2003b)

The last factor is especially relevant for social work with volunteers, as the most prevalent types of experiences tend to be short-term direct services to people in immediate need, such as the provision of emergency food, shelter, and clothing (Billingsley & Caldwell, 1994; Cnaan & Boddie, 2001). Several scholars assert, however, that if the right conditions existed, more people would be willing to participate in volunteer experiences that require prolonged amounts of time and energy (see, e.g., Billingsley, 1999; Stebbins, 1996; Wineburg, 1994).

SUMMARY

Of primary importance in this chapter is the notion that volunteerism is a complex phenomenon that is affected by the interaction of many individual and societal factors. Social workers must take into account an array of unique contextual, behavioral, social, religious, and political variables in order to effectively partner with volunteers. This leads to the subject matter of the next chapter—the main reasons why people volunteer.

DISCUSSION QUESTIONS AND LEARNING EXERCISES

1. Describe the experiences in your life that led you to want to become a social worker. Now ask someone you know to describe what led him or her to become a volunteer. What are the similarities? What are the differences?
2. This chapter suggests that religious beliefs and practices play an important role in understanding volunteerism. Do you agree? Explain why you agree or disagree.
3. Make a list of social work practice areas. Now pick one and conduct a brief study to determine how that area of practice originated. Try to find one that was not preceded by volunteerism.
4. Think of someone you consider a dedicated volunteer. Describe some of the reasons you picked him or her. Which of the ways of defining volunteer commitment in the chapter accounts for more of the reasons you consider that person a dedicated volunteer? Are any of the reasons you described excluded from the definition of active and sustained commitment? Explain your answer.
5. Think about experiences from your social work practice or from your field placement or internship. Try to think of a situation where clients served by your program would not benefit from assistance by volunteers or becoming volunteers themselves. Now explain all the ways the clients served by your program would benefit from assistance by volunteers or by becoming volunteers themselves.

2

Why People Volunteer

AS A SOCIAL WORKER, AVA HARRINGTON WORKS FOR A COMMUNITY MENTAL health center as an aftercare specialist in a substance abuse treatment program for pregnant women. The treatment program consists of six weeks of intensive outpatient group treatment, a year of monthly follow-up groups, and aftercare placement with volunteer women who serve as mentors. It is Ava's responsibility to recruit, screen, and train mentors and assign them to clients who successfully complete the treatment. The mentors provide clients with healthy friendships, access to other positive supports, support through the remainder of their pregnancies, and assistance with child rearing for six months after the children are born. As mentors they also participate in the monthly follow-up groups with clients.

Ava has developed an extensive screening and training process for potential mentors. Volunteers must fill out an application form, sign a confidentiality form, pass a background check and a urine drug screen, and show proof that their immunizations are up to date. Training is provided in several different workshops, including sessions on personal safety and confidentiality, CPR/first aid, basic drug education, and basic parenting skills. Ava offers the training every other month. She also holds an award ceremony after each round of training. Women who complete the screening and training receive a certificate. Ava needs to recruit and train a large number of volunteers because the program serves approximately seventy-five to eighty-five clients each year.

Raymond Edwards is a social worker who works for Advocates Health Project as a volunteer coordinator. Advocates Health Project is an agency that provides case management and hospice services for individuals diagnosed with HIV/AIDS as well as prevention services. As the volunteer coordinator, Raymond is responsible for recruiting, screening, training, and assigning volunteers. Raymond has also developed and leads a three-hour workshop on working with people who have HIV/AIDS.

Volunteers at Advocates Health Project perform a number of different functions. Most of the volunteers are assigned by case managers to provide clients with companionship, transportation, and assistance with day-to-day activities such as cleaning, cooking, and shopping. Other volunteers help in the office and to organize annual fund-raisers. Raymond asks volunteers who want to be assigned to clients to make at least a one-year commitment to the agency. He does not want volunteers to develop rapport with clients only to leave them shortly thereafter. He assigns those who cannot make a one-year commitment to either assist in the office or help with a fund-raiser. By distinguishing between activities that require different levels of commitment, Raymond hopes to provide volunteer opportunities for as many people as possible. On occasion, people begin working in the office and then decide they want to begin working with clients. In the same way, after spending over a year working with clients, some people decide they want to work in the office or help with a fund-raiser before they are assigned to new clients.

Duane Wellington, a social work administrator with the Department of Social Services, has been asked by the pastor of his church to organize a mission trip to Seattle. The pastor explains that a church in Seattle wants to start a drop-in center for single parents in need of last-minute day care. The church recently bought a small abandoned storefront church in downtown Seattle that is in need of major renovations before the center can open. The pastor tells Duane another church has donated all the supplies and materials needed for the renovation. A crew of about forty volunteers is needed to go for a week to work on the renovations.

*   Duane is a deacon of his church and has experience organizing mission trips. He calls his friend Shawn Collins from his Sunday school class to help him develop a plan. Shawn helped Duane organize a successful mission trip to Venezuela two years ago. He and Shawn reserve a charter bus and make arrangements at a motel a few blocks away from the building. If four people share a room, they estimate it will cost $540 for each volunteer to travel to Seattle and spend the week working on the building. Now all they have to do is recruit forty volunteers and raise enough money for the trip.*

Although Ava, Raymond, and Duane work in different practice settings, they are each responsible for finding people who want to volunteer. Ava's and Raymond's professional roles involve screening, training, and assigning volunteers to work with clients at their agencies. They have each developed extensive processes for screening, training, and assigning volunteers to ensure that people are well prepared; however, their measure of success and effectiveness is determined primarily by their ability to recruit and retain volunteers. Stated differently, Ava and Raymond could have the most elaborate procedures in place for preparing volunteers, but if there are not enough people to volunteer, some women in Ava's program may not be assigned mentors and some clients in Raymond's program may not be paired with volunteers.

As deacon at his church, Duane Wellington's responsibilities are distinctively different from Ava's and Raymond's. Whereas the other two are working in their professional roles, Duane is a volunteer in a leadership position at his church. Duane is looking for people to volunteer for a one-time, one-week activity as opposed to the others, who need to find people to volunteer for an extended period of time. Also, whereas Ava and Raymond have to find volunteers, the church congregation has probably provided Duane with a list of potential candidates. Because he is organizing volunteers in his church, the process for screening volunteers is probably much more informal, and little or no training is necessary. In fact, he will likely invite anyone to volunteer regardless of ability. Still, the success of the mission trip is dependent upon his recruitment of forty volunteers.

Social work practice with volunteers involves two basic but crucial factors—recruiting volunteers and retaining volunteers. Understanding why people volunteer is the key to effective recruitment and retention. As the three vignettes demonstrate, programs that depend on volunteers must find and maintain a large enough group of people who are committed to the mission and work of the programs.

This chapter examines the main reasons people volunteer. Although many of the reasons overlap, they are presented in two main categories: reasons people begin volunteering and reasons people continue volunteering for a sustained period of time.

WHY PEOPLE BEGIN VOLUNTEERING

There are six reasons why people begin volunteering. Before we discuss the reasons, a brief review of the underlying theory will explain how the six motivations were derived.

The six reasons for volunteering come from the functional theory of psychology, which seeks to understand the intrapersonal and interpersonal needs, goals, plans, and motives that people attempt to satisfy through their beliefs and behaviors. Functional theorists posit that there are several basic psychological functions involved in all human activity (Katz, 1960; Smith, Bruner, & White, 1956). Beliefs and behaviors that help people understand the world serve a knowledge function, those that allow people to express and act on important values serve a values function, and those that protect the ego from threatening aspects of the self serve an ego defensive function. In addition, beliefs and behaviors that lead to rewards and allow people to minimize risk serve a utilitarian function, and those that help people fit in with others serve a social adjusting function.

Viewed within the context of functional theory, understanding why people begin volunteering is no different from understanding why people get dressed in the morning, get married, exercise, participate in religious worship, or write books. We can understand these behaviors by examining the motivations behind them. Thus several broad assumptions underlie the reasons people begin volunteering: that people begin volunteering to satisfy personal needs, that different people may do the same volunteer activity to satisfy different personal needs, that people may satisfy more than one personal need with the same volunteer activity, and that the more opportunities are created for people to meet different types of personal needs, the greater is the likelihood that people will begin volunteering (Clary & Snyder, 1991).

The Six Reasons

One reason people begin volunteering centers on the opportunity volunteering offers people to express values that are important to them. Of those important values, altruistic and humanitarian concerns appear to be most frequently associated with volunteering. People who are concerned for others are the most likely to begin volunteering (Anderson & Moore, 1978; Cnaan & Goldberg-Glen, 1991). They are also more likely to volunteer in a variety of settings and participate in activities that require extended periods of service (Clary & Miller, 1986; Clary & Orenstein, 1991). Likewise, having little or no concern for others can distinguish people who have never volunteered from people who have volunteered at least once (Allen & Rushton, 1983; Dye, Goodman, Roth, Bley, & Jensen, 1973).

The second reason people begin volunteering involves the desire to have new learning experiences and exercise knowledge, skills, and abilities that might otherwise go unpracticed. Related to Katz's (1960) and Smith, Bruner, and White's (1956) knowledge function, people who volunteer are often interested in self-development through a variety of learning experiences that they could not get doing other activities (Gidron, 1978; Penner & Finkelstein, 1998). Offering volunteer opportunities that provide many chances for people to learn new skills and information increases the likelihood that an organization will attract volunteers. In the same way, volunteer opportunities that give people a chance to apply information and skills they already have attract volunteers.

People also begin volunteering to increase and reinforce their social networks. Volunteering offers opportunities for participants to meet new people, strengthen friendships, and enhance their social status by engaging in activities that are often viewed favorably by others. Increasing and reinforcing social networks is clearly related to Katz's (1960) and Smith, Bruner, and White's (1956) social adjusting function. It has also figured prominently in research on volunteering, including a study by Morrow-Howell, Kinnevy, and Mann (1999) that found that older people who volunteer report more benefits in terms of socialization, feelings of well-being, and generativity than do people of the same age participating in other social activities. Social workers who appreciate how important socializing is to potential volunteers and create work environments that promote interaction among volunteers as well as between volunteers and paid staff are likely to recruit the most people.

The fourth reason for volunteering is the career-related benefits that may result from engaging in volunteer work. Related to the utilitarian function described by

Katz (1960), some people begin volunteering in order to progress in their current career or explore a new career. Jenner (1982) and Sibicky (1992) found that a significant percentage of people begin volunteering to advance in their careers (15% and 19%, respectively). Of the people who start volunteering for career reasons, the ones who continue usually do so for one of the other five reasons or tend to stop volunteering within a short amount of time.

The final two reasons people begin volunteering are closer to the roots of classical functional theory in that both are thought to be associated with the functioning of the ego (Katz, 1960; Smith et al., 1956). First, ego defense reasons center on protecting the ego from negative features of the self. For example, volunteering may serve to reduce guilt about being more fortunate than others and may be a way to address personal problems. In contrast to the protective concern of eliminating negative aspects surrounding the ego, people may also begin volunteering to improve their sense of self-worth (Clary & Snyder, 1991). For example, some people report that volunteering is a way for them to cope with feelings of isolation, uselessness, and hopelessness. Other people report that they volunteer as a way of maintaining their mental health and increasing their self-esteem and self-confidence (Anderson & Moore, 1978; Cnaan & Goldberg-Glen, 1991).

Applying the Six Reasons

Ava and Raymond could take the six reasons into consideration as they develop strategies to recruit volunteers. Perhaps they could develop ways to deliver public education about their respective programs. To reach the widest audience, they should try to offer the information in different formats. For example, they could provide seminars in the community, invite people to open house events at their agencies, and write press releases to radio stations and television studios to promote their programs as a public service and to advertise their need for volunteers. When they give a public seminar or host an open house, they should make sure they invite some of their volunteers to attend and participate. Having volunteers organize or give the seminar could be even more effective.

In developing their seminars, it seems important that they include certain information related to the six reasons for volunteering. For instance, Ava could provide information about the especially pervasive social problems caused by substance abuse among women who are pregnant. She could share how her program addresses the problems by helping expectant mothers become drug-free and prepared to care for their children. She could also discus how volunteers play an important role by providing mentorship for their clients and describe the work involved. She could emphasize how people who volunteer in the program are seen as part of the service team. As such, they are invited to all treatment meetings and staff get-togethers. In addition, she could tell potential volunteers that the agency offers monthly training workshops in the evenings that volunteers are encouraged to attend. In the same way, Raymond can offer seminars on HIV/AIDS and the services provided by Advocates Health Project. He too should make sure he describes the important roles volunteers play, the opportunities for different trainings, and the chances to interact with paid staff and other volunteers.

Ava and Raymond may also want to find ways to express their appreciation for people who are considering volunteering for career reasons. When talking with the public, they should consider bringing someone from their staff who used to volunteer for the agency. It would also be a good idea for them to develop relationships with local universities. If the universities have social work programs, they may be able to work out field internships. Oftentimes social work courses require students to complete a number of volunteer hours. They should get to know the instructors teaching the courses and share with them the interesting opportunities they have for students to volunteer. They should not forget students in other majors who may take an elective requiring volunteer work. As more and more schools include service learning in their general education curriculum, Ava and Raymond are likely to find an abundance of potential candidates. If they want to hold onto people who begin volunteering for career reasons, however, they will need to find ways to get volunteers involved as soon as possible and as much as possible. Otherwise many of them may not continue.

There are certain things Duane could do to take the six reasons into account in his search for volunteers as well. First, he could approach people both inside and outside the church who are either single parents or know single parents and would appreciate the importance of last-minute day care. Second, he should invite people who have friends and acquaintances at the church in Seattle. He could let the community know that he needs people with different abilities and kinds of experience. He should invite people who have experience with construction and renovations and people who have never even picked up a hammer but would like to learn how to use one. He also should invite people who have experience going on mission trips and people who have never been on one. When he talks with potential volunteers, he should communicate to them how much fun they will have working and playing together. He should share how he plans for the group to sightsee one day, enjoy another day at a sporting event, and attend a Wednesday evening service with members of the church in Seattle. People will then know they will have an opportunity to meet new people and to socialize.

WHY PEOPLE CONTINUE VOLUNTEERING

As vital as it is to recruit people to volunteer, it is equally important to develop strategies to keep as many of them as possible. It would be very frustrating and costly to expend resources to recruit volunteers only to have the majority leave after a short time. Moreover, this is the point at which the efforts of many communities, organizations, and grassroots movements come to a halt. Although some turnover is typical in community and organization development, if there are not enough volunteers remaining to participate in the core planning and implementation, the project probably will not fulfill its purposes or will stall altogether. Therefore, a key component of effective social work practice with volunteers is identifying factors that may improve the likelihood that people will remain committed to volunteering for a sustained period of time. Just as important is the ability of social workers to assess volunteer commitment in order to plan future projects and services. There are five factors that can increase the likelihood that people will become committed volunteers. The volunteer commitment scale provides one way to assess the commitment of volunteers (Sherr, 2003b).

The Five Factors

People who are satisfied with the communication at an organization are more likely to remain volunteers than those who are not. Communication involves the quality of information flow from the organization to its volunteers. Information flow consists of several types of communication, including information about the organization in general and information about the specific job descriptions for volunteers as well as recognition and feedback given to the volunteers (Galindo-Kuhn & Guzley, 2001). When people participate in volunteer experiences that are different from what they were led to expect by the organization, they are less likely to continue (Wharton, 1991). How recognition and feedback are communicated is also important. Although, public displays of recognition such as banquets, award dinners, and other special events provide opportunities for group integration (another important factor), these are not the most effective ways of recognizing the contributions of volunteers. Informal recognition and feedback, particularly face-to-face conversations, are more strongly associated with volunteer satisfaction and commitment (Field & Johnson, 1993; Paradis & Usui, 1989). Providing informal recognition and appreciation early in the volunteer experience can affect volunteers' tenure of service at an organization (Stevens, 1991).

Scheduling and work assignments are another important dimension of volunteer satisfaction (Galindo-Kuhn & Guzley, 2001). Volunteers are more likely to be satisfied if their work assignments are conveniently scheduled. The actual work should involve adequate use of job skills and tasks that provide opportunities for self-expression. For example, volunteers who are given work assignments that challenge them and allow them to express themselves are more likely to continue volunteering (Gidron, 1983). Furthermore, scheduling a convenient time for volunteering has a direct effect on turnover (Miller, Powell, & Seltzer, 1990).

The next factor involves the sense of efficacy people can experience when they volunteer. Though closely related to the type of work assignment, this factor specifically refers to the relationships volunteers can have with the people benefiting from their services. Whether volunteers have direct contact with clients or serve in more peripheral roles, they tend to experience a sense of satisfaction when they have a sense of how effective their work is. Volunteers who feel that their participation is effecting change are more likely to describe volunteering as worthwhile and important (Miller et al., 1990). In contrast, feeling frustrated with one's ability to help others is often a reason cited for terminating volunteer work (Morrow-Howell & Mui, 1989; Sherr, 2003b; Wharton, 1991).

Another factor associated with volunteer satisfaction and commitment is the quality of support people receive from organizations. There are two primary types of support people need from organizations—training support and emotional support. Volunteers who participate in training report higher levels of satisfaction than those who do not (Galindo-Kuhn & Guzely, 2001). Organizations offering longer training sessions and a variety of training topics are also likely to have a larger number of volunteers who are satisfied and committed (Cyr & Dowrick, 1991; Paradis & Usui, 1989).

Emotional support is also associated with volunteer satisfaction and commitment. Emotional support involves the relational environment that exists among the paid staff, volunteer leadership, and the volunteers. When volunteers work with paid staff and other leaders who are willing to collaborate in problem solving, cooperate on projects, and encourage volunteer initiative and activity, volunteers are more likely to be satisfied with their experiences (Cyr & Dowrick, 1991; Paradis & Usui, 1989). However, when professional staff resist volunteer participation, view volunteers as a threat to their jobs, or attempt to work with volunteers from a position of power instead of reciprocity, volunteers tend to be less satisfied with their experiences (Ozminkowski, Supiano, & Cambell, 1991; Schwartz, 1977).

Closely related to emotional support, developing a sense of group integration is an important way to encourage people to continue volunteering. Whereas the support dimension involves the working relationships that provide volunteers with the training and emotional resources they need to do their jobs, group integration refers to the bonds that tie volunteers affectively to one another and the organization. These relationships are independent of the work, providing a social aspect of the volunteer experience that is associated with satisfaction and commitment. For example, Field and Johnson (1993) found that volunteers are more satisfied when they have contact with other volunteers and ample opportunity for social events with others aside from work assignments. Informal lunches and get-togethers with paid staff and other volunteers, Thanksgiving dinners, holiday parties, and award banquets are all great ways to build group integration. Just as effective, however, is encouraging staff to acknowledge and remember the names of volunteers when they see them in the community (Black & DiNitto, 1994).

The Volunteer Commitment Scale

The volunteer commitment scale consists of nine items that measure four indicators of active and sustained volunteer commitment: the level of internal com-

---

Figure 2.1 The volunteer commitment scale
The following statements are about your participation as a volunteer with this agency.

Please indicate your level of agreement with the following:	Strongly Disagree			Neutral			Strongly Agree
1. Being a volunteer with this agency is an important part of who I am.	1	2	3	4	5	6	7
2. I feel a strong sense of obligation toward this agency.	1	2	3	4	5	6	7
3. I could easily walk away from volunteering with this agency.	1	2	3	4	5	6	7
4. If I moved to another part of the country, it would be important for me to volunteer for an agency similar to this one.	1	2	3	4	5	6	7
5. I intend to fill a leadership role in the future as a volunteer in this agency.	1	2	3	4	5	6	7
6. Unless unforeseen changes occur in my life, I see myself volunteering for this agency one year from now.	1	2	3	4	5	6	7

7. How long have you been volunteering with this agency?
_____ year(s) and _____ month(s)
8. In the past twelve months, how many times have you done something others would consider volunteering for this agency? _____
9. In the past twelve months, how many hours did you spend volunteering for this agency? _____

---

mitment people feel toward a particular agency or organization, the length of time they have volunteered, how often they volunteer, and how long they volunteer (see figure 2.1). The level of internal commitment is assessed with six different items: the extent to which people feel that volunteering with an agency is an important part of their identity, the sense of obligation people feel toward the agency, the difficulty volunteers experience when leaving the agency, the likelihood that volunteers will volunteer for a similar agency if they move away, people's desire to become volunteer leaders at the agency, and the likelihood that people will continue to volunteer at the agency the following year, baring unforeseen circumstances. The other three indicators are assessed with one item each that asks people how long they have volunteered for the agency as well as the number of times they have volunteered elsewhere and how many hours they volunteered during the previous year.

Applying the Factors

After Ava, Raymond, and Duane do a good job of recruiting volunteers, they need to develop strategies to keep as many of them as possible. Considering the volunteer commitment factors should help them create effective strategies to do this.

There are several things they can do to maintain good communication. First, each of them should make an effort to get to know as many volunteers as possible. For Ava and Raymond especially, getting to know each and every volunteer should be considered a primary job responsibility. If there are people on their list of volunteers with whom they are unfamiliar or have not seen in awhile, they should make a special effort to contact and talk with them. Second, it is important that they have realistic expectations of the amount of time and energy needed for various tasks. Moreover, they must make sure volunteers understand exactly what each task entails. The more specific they are in describing the tasks, the more volunteers will enjoy their experiences. Third, they should take time to explain the history of the agency and the possibilities for volunteers to contribute to that history. They also need to remember to look for opportunities to show appreciation and to give feedback. Formal gatherings are still important, but they can't replace the expression of genuine thanks while volunteers are making contributions.

When it comes to actual work assignments, it is important for Ava, Raymond, and Duane to make sure volunteers are properly trained to meet their expectations. At the same time, once their volunteers are given the tools to complete a task, they should allow enough flexibility for people to carry out tasks within their own style. If some volunteers find innovative ways to complete tasks, they should take note of it and provide positive feedback. It is also important for them to find a healthy balance between change and routine. In some instances, volunteers gain confidence as they develop a routine for their activities. In other instances, doing the same thing over and over again becomes frustrating. They should consider making periodic changes in tasks and roles that are far enough apart for volunteers to gain confidence and often enough to provide new experiences. For Ava and Raymond, it is also a good idea to let volunteers have input in creating their schedules. Including them communicates respect for other areas of their lives and elicits a greater sense of ownership over the agency.

As the three assign people to different tasks, it is important that they assign tasks so that as many volunteers as possible see evidence of the good work they are doing. It is also essential for them to help volunteers set realistic expectations of success. They must teach volunteers to pay attention to small gains as well as larger ones. For people volunteering in more indirect roles, Ava and Raymond should share success stories and communicate how valuable the work of volunteers is to the staff's ability to run the program effectively and efficiently. Volunteers should also be kept abreast of new agency developments and improvements. Ava and Raymond can explain how the contributions of volunteers contribute to the improvements.

When it comes to supportive training, Ava and Raymond should consider providing opportunities for professional development for volunteers as well as staff. One option is for them to offer interesting trainings at their agencies. They could be even more creative by sending one or two volunteers away to an important training that takes a day or two. After the training, they could invite the volunteers to a staff meeting to share the information with everyone. It is also important for all three recruiters to make time for small talk with volunteers. They should give volunteers opportunities to share the highs and lows of their experiences. They could also be honest and share with them some of the highlights and problems at the agency. This is one way they can give their volunteers a chance to give and receive emotional support.

Ava, Raymond, and Duane should create opportunities for volunteers to get together outside of their primary tasks. Spending time planning formal events is effective, especially if they enlist volunteers to help organize and facilitate the events. This way, volunteers will be vested in the events and make sure other volunteers attend. Encouraging informal opportunities for staff and volunteers to mingle and socialize allows people chances to build genuine bonds of collegiality. They could create a Web site for volunteers to plan social gatherings. They could also share news of people's birthdays, anniversaries, and other types of occasions for celebration. On occasion, they could invite some of the volunteers to lunch.

Finally, Ava and Raymond should consider eliciting the help of a few volunteers to periodically administer the volunteer commitment scale to all their volunteers. If any of the volunteers have the ability, they could also ask them to help process and analyze the information. Afterwards they could work with the volunteers to use the information to plan future work assignments and develop strategies to improve the overall commitment of their volunteers.

LINKING THE REASONS WHY PEOPLE BEGIN AND CONTINUE VOLUNTEERING

In practice, many of the reasons why people begin and continue volunteering overlap. For instance, people may begin volunteering in order to learn new things and continue volunteering if they get the supportive training and work assignments that allow them to continue to learn new things. In the same way, some people begin volunteering to express important values. Having the emotional support of staff and other volunteers allows people to recognize and reflect on how they are expressing their values. Also, when volunteers witness people benefiting from their contributions, it is likely to enhance how they feel about themselves. Likewise, offering

---

Figure 2.2 Reasons people begin and continue volunteering

Reasons People Begin Volunteering
1. To express important values
2. To learn new things and use abilities
3. To increase and reinforce social networks
4. To advance a career
5. To protect ego from negative emotions
6. To enhance self-esteem and self-worth

Reasons People Continue Volunteering
1. Good communication
2. Convenient schedules and interesting work assignments
3. Visible evidence that people are benefiting
4. Training and emotional support
5. Group integration

---

different types of social gatherings enhances group integration, reinforces and expands social networks, and wards off feelings of isolation. Finally, the quality of the communication flow between staff and volunteers is central to all the other factors. The reasons why people begin and continue volunteering are summarized in figure 2.2.

OTHER REASONS WHY PEOPLE VOLUNTEER

There are additional reasons why people volunteer. First, some people volunteer to pursue a unique type of serious leisure activity. Activities are considered serious leisure when they are systematically pursued and require substantial application of special skills, knowledge, and experiences (Stebbins, 1996). In many instances, these activities involve nearly the same investment in time and energy as a second career. A primary characteristic of serious leisure activities is the vast amount of personal satisfaction people experience. This deep satisfaction offsets any frustrations people experience when they have to endure hardships, persevere through setbacks, and occasionally participate in unpleasant tasks (Parker, 1992). Chess, golf, ham radio operating, old car restoration, and home construction are examples of serious leisure activities, while taking a nap, going for a walk in the park, watching television, and reading the newspaper are more casual leisure activities. What distinguishes volunteering from other activities, however, is the emphasis on helping others rather than on gratifying self-interests. In addition, when engaging in serious leisure activities, people usually become part of an embedded social group with newsletters, events, routines, practices, and organizational structures. People who continue volunteering at Ava's and Raymond's agencies probably view their actions as serious leisure.

Many people also volunteer to express or act on their religious beliefs. In nearly all religious traditions, volunteering is seen as one way of expressing the core belief of stewardship (Wolfer & Sherr, 2003). In general, stewardship involves the use of the time, talent, and wealth of individuals to serve the greater needs of the community. The belief in the importance of stewardship is usually expressed both in and outside religious congregations. In fact, oftentimes the most active and committed volunteers are also the most active members of their religious congregations (Sherr & Shields, 2005). Therefore, it would be wise for Ava, Raymond, and Duane to recruit volunteers at places of worship, where they are likely to find an abundance of people willing to consider becoming volunteers. Moreover, the three of them may want to consider sharing the names of potential volunteers. It's quite possible that the people who are interested in going on the mission trip might also be interested in volunteering at one of the agencies. In the same way, people volunteering for Ava and Raymond might be interested in going on the mission trip.

Cultural values also influence why people volunteer and the kinds of tasks they are willing to undertake. Cultural values are the accumulation of norms, principles, and rules that guide the behavior of people who share a common language and environment. Three overlapping and competing sets of cultural values exert a direct and significant influence on volunteerism: emphasizing individual well-being as opposed to group well-being, mastering the social environment as opposed to fitting into the social environment, and preserving social order as opposed to promoting egalitarian principles. In the United States and most of Europe, there is an emphasis on individual autonomy, concern for others, and individual growth from succeeding or mastering the social environment (Penner, 2000). The constellation of these cultural values tends to reinforce volunteerism as a way to simultaneously express individual uniqueness and concern for others' welfare and improve oneself through activity in the community. At the same time, preserving social order and group well-being still remains important, creating a paradox that makes it easier to recruit volunteers for certain activities and more difficult to recruit for others.

For instance, Ava, Raymond, and Duane are likely to be successful recruiting volunteers because they are seeking people for direct service roles focused on helping other individuals improve their well-being. If, however, Ava wanted volunteers to help with an advocacy campaign to increase state or federal funding for better substance abuse treatment, she would probably find it more difficult to recruit people. In the same way, Duane would find it more difficult to recruit volunteers to go to Seattle to take part in an advocacy campaign to lobby for equal wages for minorities and women. In both cases, it would be more difficult because they would be asking people to participate in activities that have more potential to disrupt the social order and challenge the policies, values, and practices embedded in the culture. However, as social workers, they still should focus on involving volunteers in activities that promote systemic social and economic justice. Although it is more challenging to recruit people for such efforts, this does not mean it is impossible. In fact, as we will discuss in chapter 10, part of this process is engaging volunteers in direct service roles and cultivating relationships in which a significant number can be educated and mobilized to address underlying social problems when the opportunity arises.

SUMMARY

In order to recruit and retain volunteers, social workers must understand the reasons why people volunteer. Incorporating recruitment strategies that offer people opportunities to express their values, learn new things, build social networks, advance their careers, and enhance their self-esteem can help social workers recruit more volunteers. If social workers want to develop effective partnerships with volunteers, they need to maintain good communication, create flexible assignments, put volunteers in positions where they can observe the success of the people they are serving, provide training and support, and plan activities that enhance group integration. In the next chapter, we will examine volunteerism through the lens of different human behavior theories.

DISCUSSION QUESTIONS AND LEARNING EXERCISES

1. According to functional theory, the reasons people begin volunteering are similar to the reasons they engage in any activity. Do you agree? Explain why you agree or disagree.
2. Compare a grassroots movement or community project that is thriving in your area with one that has lost its momentum. What are some of the main differences? Find out how many volunteers are involved in the one that is thriving as opposed to the one that is not. Interview at least one person involved in the successful project. Try to identify ways in which the project is able to retain so many volunteers.
3. Think of an activity or a hobby you take very seriously. How much time do you spend reading about it? How often does it come up in conversation? Describe the social world in which you're a part because of your interest in this hobby or activity. If you can't think of an activity or hobby, ask someone else about his or hers.
4. Visit a local service at a synagogue, church, mosque, or temple. Locate the people most involved in the service. Talk with some of them to find out all the ways they volunteer inside and outside their religious congregation.
5. Describe some of the ways you would recruit and retain volunteers at the agency where you work or do your field placement. Try to incorporate all factors mentioned in the chapter as part of your strategy.

3

Volunteerism and Human Behavior Theory

NOW THAT WE HAVE ESTABLISHED A WORKING DEFINITION OF VOLUNTEER-ism and explored the reasons why people volunteer, a few points should be clear. Volunteerism involves much more then working without pay; it involves people making choices to do things to help society in ways that go beyond their basic obligations. People begin and continue volunteering for many different reasons. Although there is great individual-to-individual variability, it is important for social workers to understand and take into consideration as many of the reasons as possible in their strategies to recruit and retain committed volunteers. Moreover, working with volunteers begins with appreciating the complex nature of volunteerism.

This chapter analyzes volunteerism through the lens of eight different human behavior theories. From a strengths perspective, volunteerism provides an opportunity to consider these theories without advancing a view of individuals, groups, and communities as pathological or deviant. Instead, volunteerism encourages individual capacity building while simultaneously addressing community social problems. The vignettes from chapters 1 and 2 will illustrate how human behavior theories apply to volunteerism.

WHAT ARE HUMAN BEHAVIOR THEORIES?

The theories covered in this chapter have a few things in common. First, they are sets of interrelated statements designed to explain and guide observed patterns of human behavior. Second, social workers can use these theories as tools to interpret behaviors and develop interventions and strategies. As theories, however, they are all provisional, meaning it is possible that future scientific inquiry could lead to modified or even totally contradictory statements about the same human behavior. For current purposes, the theories that are presented here represent the most common perspectives social workers use to understand human behavior.

SYSTEMS THEORY AND THE ECOLOGICAL PERSPECTIVE

Systems theory originated from the fields of sociology and biology. In social work, individuals, groups, and communities are all considered human systems comprised of other interrelated systems. On one hand, human systems are whole systems with boundaries that give them their own identities. On the other hand, all human systems are also subsystems of other larger systems. The systems interrelate to fulfill different functions. For instance, individuals are made up of biological systems, emotional systems, cognitive systems, and spiritual systems. These systems interact and function in a way that allows individuals to survive and coexist with other individuals. Likewise, group systems consist of several individuals who interrelate to fulfill different functions for the group. In the same way, individuals and groups belong to larger systems (Hutchison, 2003; Turner, 1986).

Human systems interact with one another and with their environments through constant and dynamic transactions of inputs and outputs. The ecological perspective is a theoretical framework used to describe the transactions between people and their environments. Goodness of fit is a key concept characterizing these transactions. As people and environments go through an adaptation process, the adaptation process can be positive or negative, depending on the nature of the transaction. When transactions are sufficient and reciprocal, a goodness of fit exists. Insufficient or excessively harmful transactions make life more stressful for both people and environments (Germain & Bloom, 1999). Social workers aim to provide sufficient resources and remove barriers in order to improve goodness of fit for as many people as possible (National Association of Social Workers, 1999).

Volunteerism is one way reciprocal transactions can occur between different systems. People who volunteer learn new things and feel helpful and needed. People receiving assistance from volunteers benefit from the services and from knowing they are important enough for others to care about. Agencies, businesses, and organizations providing opportunities for volunteerism can generate positive public relations and have enough volunteers to carry out their operations. From a community perspective, volunteering can change how people think about others, bring different cultures together, and foster an overall feeling of participation and trust among community members. In other words, volunteerism allows opportunities for a greater diversity of inputs and outputs, which is important for enhancing goodness of fit.

When Daryl Reynolds tutors adolescents in math, several things occur that promote goodness of fit. Interacting with the children at the Boys and Girls Club helps him maintain his love for mathematics. Seeing the children learn also inspires him and brings him joy and affirms his ability to teach others. His interactions also expose him to children and families from different backgrounds. Significant to social workers, his exposure brings him in touch with the larger social issues surrounding the reasons why many of these children need a tutor from the Boys and Girls Club in the first place.

At the same time, the children working with Daryl benefit in several ways. First, the children learn math skills that they need to function in society. As the children learn, they gain self-confidence and experience success at school, and their success opens up opportunities for them to attend college or learn a trade in the future. Second, the children benefit socially by interacting with a positive male role model who cares for them. Although math is the main reason they meet with Daryl, the children could talk to him about other things as well if they need to. Third, through Daryl the children have access to an expanded social network, as Daryl eventually uses his network to create a positive transaction between his company and the Boys and Girls Club (two larger systems) to build a computer lab for the children.

As Daryl tutors and brokers a transaction between his company and the club, other larger systems may be affected. For instance, the school system may refer more students to the club. The club may begin looking for additional volunteers to help run the computer lab. The media may do a story on the new computer lab, giving Daryl's company positive exposure. Other companies in his community may decide to get involved with the club or with other agencies. At some point, someone (perhaps a social worker) could organize a partnership to improve the math and computer competencies of children in the community. The partnership could raise funds to create additional facilities, invite local colleges and universities to participate, and lobby state policy makers to improve the math curriculum at public schools or create incentives for other large companies to get involved.

CONFLICT THEORY

The roots of contemporary conflict theory can be traced to Karl Marx and Friedrich Engels (1848/1955). For them, conflict is desirable because it sets in motion social action to promote social justice. Therefore, conflict theory stands in direct contrast to systems theory. Whereas systems theory assumes that each system serves a function and interacts with other systems to achieve and maintain goodness of fit, conflict theory assumes that stability and harmonious functioning are unusual. Conflict, coercion, and change are considered the normal state of interactions between human systems (or social structures). To conflict theorists, goodness of fit is an elusive ideal that changes constantly as different interest groups compete for the authority to advance the values and positions that define social structures (Dahrendorf, 1959).

Three overlapping concepts are central to conflict theory—power, surplus value, and subjection. Power is the ability to frame ideas and influence the decisions and actions of other people. Conflict theorists primarily focus on power relationships to understand how people use power to create and resist change (Blalock, 1989). People use and maintain power by promoting their viewpoints and by controlling the means of production. As some interest groups gain prominence and the ability to influence social structures, they exercise control over groups that hold different views to create the best fit for themselves. In the same way, groups of people who own the means of production maintain authority because their economic advantage provides them with better access to other sources of power such as education and political influence. The control of production is connected to the concept of surplus value. Surplus value refers to the difference between the selling price of an item or service and the cost of labor. The larger the surplus value, the easier it is for the few people controlling the means of production to maintain power. As a group of people maintains power, a larger number have less time, energy, and financial resources to fully participate in contributing to the rules, norms, and mores of the social environment. Thus, subjection tends to occur where larger groups of people become estranged and powerless from the process of creating and changing social conditions (Dahrendorf, 1959).

In contemplating how conflict theory applies to volunteerism, we must examine volunteerism in relation to these concepts. For instance, how does volunteerism influence power, and vice versa? On one hand, people who volunteer come from nearly every demographic group. Volunteerism provides people, regardless of age, gender, education level, marital status, and socioeconomic level, with an opportunity to participate in the community. In other words, volunteerism allows people with access to different amounts and types of power to interact with each other for common purposes. Their interaction could lead to social action that addresses social justice. On the other hand, who shapes the parameters of volunteerism in terms of leadership, the focus of volunteering efforts, and the types of activities in which people engage when they volunteer? Studies of who volunteers in America reveal that people with higher incomes are more likely to volunteer. In addition, white men and women who work, have finished college, and live in two-parent households are the most likely to volunteer (U.S. Department of Labor, 2005). Although social workers could use volunteerism to influence current power relationships to promote social justice, currently it seems that people with power control the parameters of volunteerism.

Two other questions are interrelated: Is there surplus value from volunteer labor, and does volunteerism deter or contribute to subjection? When a nonprofit organization uses volunteers to deliver services, it is cost effective, allowing the organization's financial resources to stretch further. When large corporations encourage their employees to volunteer, positive relationships with stakeholders and other potential consumers are created that allow the corporations to sell more products. Volunteerism can be used to deter or contribute to subjection. In some ways, providing volunteer assistance to people who need help can provide just enough support to siphon the will of disenfranchised people to prevent them from having a greater voice in the community. As demonstrated in the next section, however, volunteerism can also create critical awareness among enough people to lead to collective action.

As a loan officer for Southland Mortgage, Aaron Freeman is required to join a volunteer association. Although the business owner pays the membership fees, in some ways the amount of time Aaron spends as a volunteer adds to the surplus value by stretching out the number of hours he is working for the mortgage company. As he spends time attending lunches and participating in community service projects, he is simultaneously working to develop relationships that could lead to additional business. The fact that the business owner encouraged Aaron to become a member of the Lions Club rather than to fulfill the volunteer requirement through a social service agency is also noteworthy. Membership dues for a volunteer organization such as the Lions Club can be relatively expensive (in some cases over $1,000 annually). The dues help ensure that the people Aaron interacts with at the meetings either are wealthy enough that they can afford to pay the dues on their own or work for a company that can pay it for them. Thus the dues limit access to the Lions Club for people of lower socioeconomic status. When interactions do occur between the club's volunteers and the community, the club decides what population will receive assistance and how that assistance will be provided.

EMPOWERMENT THEORY

Empowerment theory builds upon the concepts of conflict theory by formulating strategies to reduce or eliminate the exploitive conditions in the social environment. In general, empowerment refers to a process by which people, organizations, and communities gain power to have mastery over their affairs and participate in the political processes of their communities and employing institutions (Rappaport, 1987). Whereas conflict theorists focus more on the coercion and subjection that occur as a result of authority and those who control the means of production, empowerment theorists focus on the processes that lead to social stratification. Social stratification refers to the process by which people are grouped hierarchically based on inequalities in wealth, power, and prestige as well as gender, age, race, ethnicity, disability, religion, and sexual orientation (Robbins, Chatterjee, & Canda, 1998).

Empowerment and conflict theorists share an awareness of the influence that power relationships can have on efforts to resist and initiate structural change in social systems. In addition, both theories share the belief that change only occurs when there are enough people to create a collective action that forces power relationships to be renegotiated. Empowerment theorists, however, also recognize that collective action begins and is maintained through the development of individual awareness that a change is possible and desirable. Stated differently, collective action must grow out of living experiences shared by individuals who are willing to work together to address a common social problem. The process of individuals sharing information and collective experiences related to a social problem is called raising critical consciousness (Lee, 1994).

Generally, clubs like the Lions Club tend to choose to participate in community events and social issues that are politically neutral, such as providing people with eyeglasses, creating parks, participating in parades, and beautifying historic neighborhoods (Charles, 1993). What if, however, some of the members were social workers who viewed educating and channeling the clubs to provide community service concerning other social problems as an important part of their work? For instance, what if Ava Harrington became a member of the same club as Aaron Freeman? As she developed rapport with the members, she could educate them about the growing number of pregnant women with substance abuse issues in the community. She could teach them about the various factors that surround the issue, such as poverty, domestic violence, and race and gender discrimination. She could eventually persuade the club to sponsor community events to raise money for the agency, ask other female members to become mentors, or even facilitate a coalition between her agency and the club. In other words, she could use her knowledge of empowerment theory to develop collective action to address the issues surrounding pregnant women with substance abuse issues in her community.

How does Ava transform her membership into opportunities to recruit volunteers and raise overall awareness of pregnant women with substance abuse issues? She has to remember that it will probably take some time—perhaps months or even years. With that in mind, there are several important steps Ava can take. First, when she attends meetings or participates in community service projects, she does so as a genuine volunteer (Sherr, 2003b). She takes time getting to know all the members, listening to their stories of how they became volunteers and why they continue. She learns to appreciate the various reasons they volunteer and embraces their dual desire to develop business opportunities and personal friendships as well as contribute to the community. She also takes time to learn the informal and formal cultural rules of the group. Second, in casual conversations with other volunteers, she talks about her work experiences. She is also attentive to verbal and nonverbal cues from others who may want to share their experiences. Most likely, other volunteers will have some knowledge of people with substance abuse issues.

Third, as she develops genuine relationships with more and more volunteers, she offers to give a presentation about the issue to the club at one of the lunch meetings. Perhaps she brings a current volunteer mentor to help her explain some of the needs of the women in the community and share some of her program's success stories. Fourth, after the presentation, she begins talking with the leaders of the club, who are always looking for new community service projects, about opportunities for members to begin working with her agency. She tells them about opportunities for fund-raising, direct volunteering, and co-sponsoring community events.

Finally, during her entire time as a volunteer, she tells colleagues at work about how much she enjoys the club and the service projects she works on, and she invites some of them to come to a meeting as her guests. She also talks to her administrators about the possibility for collaboration between the club and the agency. She tells them about all the community leaders who volunteer with her, their abilities, and their access to other resources. Perhaps she even offers to set up a meeting with the leaders of the club and the administrators to develop a partnership. In the end, she will have raised the critical consciousness of the club members about the social problem of substance abuse among pregnant women and created the opportunity for collective action.

PHENOMENOLOGICAL THEORY

Raising critical consciousness occurs through a process of shaping the meaning of all the cultural, situational, and contextual realities people experience. As a group of people share their experiences, the similarities and differences help the group construct a collective reality. Phenomenological theory helps explain how constructed realities develop.

Phenomenology originated in the study of theology and philosophy. When applied to social work, it refers to the process of people interpreting the meaning of events and how those events fit with their lives. Phenomenology encompasses an analysis of history, culture, and individual and group perspectives that influence how people define their existence. From a phenomenological view, people are constantly working out who they are and evaluating how they fit with their own sense of what it means to live a worthwhile and decent life (Taylor, 1989). Phenomenological theorists posit that norms, attitudes, groups, and social institutions are not independent, factual entities (Berger & Luckman, 1967; Husserl, 1970; Schutz, 1967). Rather, people construct a shared reality through social interactions with each other. As people interact, they can modify the meanings of events for others or change the meaning of events for themselves. Complete reliance on phenomenological theory to explain human behavior can result in hopeless relativism, as ultimately there can be no right or wrong. Nevertheless, a tempered application of the theory is useful because it reminds social workers to examine the unique social context of every individual, group, and community. Understanding the uniqueness of social context is especially important for social work with volunteers.

People have very different life experiences. The social context of someone growing up on a farm in southwest Iowa is quite different from that of someone growing up in downtown Los Angeles. In the same way, volunteerism occurs in many different social contexts. The social context for volunteering at a homeless shelter is probably much different from that of volunteering at a fire department. Moreover, individuals from the same location, culture, or family can ascribe different meanings to similar living experiences. Likewise, people who volunteer may have different reasons for doing the same type of work at the same organization. As in other fields of social work practice, it is important to assess and appreciate all the circumstances involved in working with volunteers. For Ava Harrington and Raymond Edwards, the ability to recruit and retain committed volunteers depends on understanding and appreciating the unique reasons people may volunteer for their agencies. It is just as important, however, for Ava and Raymond to understand and appreciate the history, culture, and norms of their respective agencies.

Consistent with a phenomenological view, volunteerism is also a practical way of helping people find new or more relevant meaning in their lives. Before Estella Gomez's husband died, she spent most of her time at home with her daughter and traveling with her husband. After her husband died, she participated in a bereavement support group at the hospice. The group expanded her immediate community to several other people who had lost a spouse. At the group, she met Melissa, and they began spending time together shopping and going to the country club. Eventually, Estella became a hospice volunteer working with families and making presentations about hospice in the community. Her unique experiences as someone faced with the impending death of her husband, the mother of a child who no longer lives in the home, and the recipient of hospice services all contributed to her decision to become a volunteer. At the same time, it appears that becoming a hospice volunteer has given Estella renewed meaning as she spends time volunteering every week.

SOCIAL LEARNING THEORY

Social learning theory developed as an outgrowth of classical behaviorism. In addition to the belief that behavior is shaped by antecedent conditions and consequences, social learning theorists focus on thoughts, expectations, emotions, and stresses that influence learned behaviors. Modeling and imitation are the central processes of social learning theory. Modeling and imitation are processes where people can learn new behavior or change their current behavior by observing the behavior of others. Modeling behavior can have three distinct effects on observing individuals. When someone engages in a behavior, it may invoke an imitative response in which observing individuals repeat the same behavior, strengthen or weaken a previously learned behavior, or prompt a previously acquired response behavior (Bandura & Walters, 1963).

As people observe more and more behaviors and then engage in response behaviors, they develop a sense of self-efficacy. Self-efficacy is a key concept of social learning theory that refers to the confidence people gain about their ability to master an activity. Moreover, as people develop a sense of self-efficacy in one area of living, it often has an effect on other areas and results in a sense of efficacy expectation. Efficacy expectation is a similar key concept of social learning theory that refers to people gaining an expectation about their ability to accomplish larger, more involved tasks (Bandura, 1977, 1986).

Social learning theory provides a useful framework for conceptualizing volunteerism. Family and friends are often the paths by which people come to volunteer. By hearing stories from their mothers and fathers and being brought along as children, individuals often develop an expectation that they too will volunteer. Likewise, individuals who have colleagues at work who volunteer and talk about their experiences are more likely to consider volunteering. When individuals volunteer, their behavior is reinforced by the people they are working with. The longer people volunteer, the more willing they become to try other types of volunteer service because they have developed a sense of self-efficacy from their previous experience. Some individuals gain enough confidence from their experiences to assume leadership responsibilities as volunteers. For children and adolescents, developing self-efficacy by volunteering is associated with attending college, earning higher degrees, socializing more with people from different racial and ethnic groups, and being more likely to continue volunteering as an adult (Astin, Sax, & Avalos, 1999; Spacapan & Oskamp, 1992).

In planning the mission trip for his church, several factors related to the social learning theory will help Duane Wellington recruit volunteers. First, he and his friend Shawn have organized a successful mission trip in the past. They both have a sense of efficacy about planning the current trip. Second, the pastor of the church personally asked him to organize the mission trip. As the leader of the church, the pastor makes known his belief that the trip is important and his expectation that people in the church will respond to the call for volunteers. Furthermore, the pastor can use his position to encourage people who attend worship services to consider participating. In the same way, the pastor has probably established an understanding that engaging in mission trips is an important part of the church's function and a way for people to express their beliefs.

The members of the church can also help Duane. There are probably a number of people in the church who have some experience with construction. If he knows in advance the types of jobs that will need to be filled to complete the renovations, he can ask people with similar experience to consider volunteering. In the same way, there are probably many people in the church who have been on mission trips. He could invite them to come on the trip or ask them to talk with other church members about their positive experiences on mission trips in the past. Finally, Duane can work with the pastor to encourage everyone in the church, whether they can volunteer or not, to help raise enough funds to pay for the trip. People who have attended the church for an extended amount of time probably expect to contribute to the mission fund because of their experiences with other mission activities in the past.

LIFE SPAN THEORY AND LIFE COURSE THEORY

Life span theory and life course theory are two different ways of explaining how human behavior develops and changes throughout the life cycle. Both theories view human development as a complex interaction of physiological, psychological, social, and spiritual processes. Life span theory is based on a psychological perspective emphasizing the physical and personality development of individuals, which occurs in clearly defined age-related stages. Life course theory is based more on a sociological perspective emphasizing the influence of shared history and culture (Robbins et al., 1998).

Life span theory is rooted in Freud's (1905/1953) theory of the psychosexual stages of childhood development; Erikson's (1963) work, however, is considered

Figure 3.1 Erikson's eight stages of the life cycle

Stage 1 (birth-1 year)	Trust versus mistrust
Stage 2 (ages 2-3)	Autonomy versus shame and doubt
Stage 3 (ages 3-5)	Initiative versus guilt
Stage 4 (ages 6-12)	Industry versus inferiority
Stage 5 (ages 12-20)	Identity versus role confusion
Stage 6 (early-late 20s)	Intimacy versus isolation
Stage 7 (late 20s-50s)	Generativity versus stagnation
Stage 8 (late adulthood)	Integrity versus despair

more influential. In addition to focusing on human development in childhood, Erikson considered human development occurring throughout adulthood. For Erikson, healthy development depended on people mastering life tasks occurring during a predictable sequence from birth to death. He developed a model of human development dividing the life cycle into eight stages (see figure 3.1).

A major critique of life span theory is that development is thought to occur across universal life stages, applying equally to all groups of people regardless of culture, socioeconomic status, gender, race, and ethnicity. Life course theory emerged to address differences in these sociological factors. Although they acknowledge the presence of typical life stages, life course theorists call attention to how history and culture affect people's experiences during each stage (Elder, 1998; George, 1993; Hareven, 2000).

A few basic concepts highlight the life course view of human development. Cohorts are groups of people who experience social changes within a given culture in the same sequence and at the same age (Setterson & Mayer, 1997). People belong to several cohorts of different sizes based on when they were born, where they live, and their perceived status. For example, a sixty-five-year-old white male corporate executive living in Manhattan, New York, belongs to different cohorts and thus has different perspectives than a twenty-eight-year-old black female homemaker living in a rural town in Georgia. Instead of the clearly defined development stages put forth in life span theory, transitions refer to changes occurring throughout the life cycle that represent a distinct departure from prior roles and statuses to a new set of roles and statuses (George, 1993). Examples of transitions include going to college, leaving home, getting married, becoming a parent, getting a first job, and receiving a promotion. Trajectories refer to long-term patterns of living that involve numerous transitions. Depending on a number of individual and environmental factors, people live their lives in multiple trajectories (i.e., educational trajectories, work trajectories, family trajectories, and health trajectories). Moreover, people can change their trajectories, especially after experiencing a significant life event. Significant life events are relatively abrupt occurrences that can produce serious and long-lasting changes in life trajectories (Holmes, 1978). Significant life events include positive events such as meeting an inspirational person or facing a challenge as well as negative events such as experiencing the death of a loved one and getting in trouble with the law.

Volunteerism is a useful phenomenon for examining life span theory and life course theory. As an action to help others that requires people to go beyond their basic obligations, volunteerism can help improve predictable life transitions. Volunteering can help teenagers develop positive self-identities and place young adults in intimate situations with a larger, more diverse group of people. By volunteering, people also can develop a sense of generativity by which they feel useful to society in a way that goes beyond their occupations. For example, volunteering significantly contributed to Daryl Reynold's and Aaron Freeman's overall quality of life. Volunteering was a significant life event for Daryl that helped him sustain his love for math and made tutoring for the Boys and Girls Club an important part of his life trajectory. In the same way, volunteering for the Lions Club simultaneously expanded Aaron's network of colleagues and allowed him to apply his business skills to serve the community through different projects organized by the club.

Volunteering can also prevent people in stressful occupations from burning out and help them maintain a healthy perspective on all the areas in their lives. This point is especially relevant for us as social workers practicing in large bureaucracies. I volunteer for the same reasons for which I initially became a social worker—to serve other people and promote social and economic justice. Volunteering also allows people in late adulthood to remain useful and active. In the process of helping others, older adults have an opportunity to reflect on what they have done in the past, make up for decisions and actions they regret, and gain an overall sense of integrity about their lives. Moreover, social workers can use volunteerism to help clients through unresolved life stages from childhood. As a part of developing treatment plans, social workers can encourage clients to volunteer in situations that provide opportunities for them to take risks, work with new people, complete tasks, improvise, and use initiative. Social workers can also help clients articulate the gains made from volunteering and apply them to other areas of their lives.

The basic concepts from the life course theory are important for organizations and staff recruiting volunteers. On one hand, organizations are more successful recruiting volunteers when they understand their history and can communicate how their history contributes to their future trajectory (Galindo-Kuhn & Guzley, 2001; Sherr, 2003b). On the other hand, it is important for staff recruiting volunteers to spend enough time listening to the stories of volunteers. Using basic social work skills such as reflective listening, probing, and clarifying, Ava Harrington and Raymond Edwards can discover why people seek opportunities to volunteer for their organizations. People may want to volunteer during a life transition or after experiencing a significant life event. For example, Duane Wellington can share with church members how volunteering for a mission trip can become a significant life event that causes them to rethink their life trajectories. The point is that Ava,

Raymond, and Duane should spend enough time listening and appreciating the stories behind why people are thinking about volunteering and help them fulfill their expectations by volunteering for their organizations.

SOCIAL EXCHANGE THEORY

Social exchange theory evolved from psychology, sociology, and economics to explain human behavior based on self-interest and choices made to accomplish personal goals. The basic premise of the theory is that people make choices to maximize rewards and minimize costs. The basic premise applies to exchanges between individuals as well as larger social systems (Blau, 1964). Rewards can be tangible (money) or intangible (attention, status, affection) so long as they are seen as having value or bringing satisfaction. Costs occur as either physical and emotional disadvantages or missed opportunities to gain rewards.

A key concept of social exchange theory is the idea of reciprocal exchange. Reciprocal exchange refers to the expectation that when people receive rewards, they respond by doing good things for others (Homans, 1974). Furthermore, reciprocal exchange involves the idea that interactions between people should remain stable. Cultural norms and laws provide parameters that guide reciprocal exchanges. In general, cultural norms and laws are upheld when large numbers of people see them as beneficial. In some circumstances, however, people may violate norms and laws when they believe the costs are too great and the rewards too small (Thibaut & Kelley, 1959).

At first glance, social exchange theory may not seem relevant to volunteerism. Why would people engage in an activity to help others without receiving remuneration? A closer look, however, shows that social exchange theory is one of the most useful perspectives for understanding volunteerism. As we discussed in chapter 2, there are many potential benefits to volunteering. Volunteering provides people with opportunities to express or demonstrate their beliefs; learn new things; fend off feelings such as guilt, shame, and isolation; and enhance their self-confidence and sense of efficacy. Although the cost of volunteering for Estella Gomez included attending workshops, showing proof that her immunizations were up to date, and working several hours a week, she probably felt that she was receiving enough rewards to continue volunteering. She likely enjoyed working with new people, learning about hospice, being productive, and perhaps feeling as if she could return the gift she received from hospice by helping others facing a terminal illness.

Volunteer commitment is directly connected to the concept of reciprocal exchanges. People become committed to volunteering with an organization when their self-interests merge with the interests and needs of the organization (Kanter, 1972; Sherr, 2003b). Over the course of a year, Aaron Freeman went from being hesitant about volunteering to being an active member of the Lions Club. From a social exchange perspective, his transition into being a committed volunteer occurred because the needs and interests of the club were congruent with his needs and interests—promoting a healthy environment for business while serving the community. As a social worker, Ava Harrington will recruit more committed volunteers if she can communicate her agency's mission and needs to people who think it is important for children to be born to parents who are alcohol- and drug-free. In the same way, the most committed volunteers for Raymond's agency will likely be people who think it is important to care for people with HIV/AIDS.

MASLOW'S THEORY OF SELF-ACTUALIZATION AND SELF-TRANSCENDENCE

Abraham Maslow (1968), a humanistic psychologist, heralded the beginning of a new movement in psychology that focused on helping people reach their potential. Instead of viewing human behavior as largely determined by unconscious, instinctual, and selfish impulses, as described by Freud, or as responding to stimuli and consequences, as described by behaviorists, Maslow focused on human strengths and the positive qualities of lovingness, spontaneity, meaningfulness, creativity, freedom, and dignity. Self-actualization and self-transcendence are two concepts that describe the process of people developing their potential. Self-actualization refers to people's natural inherent tendency to reach their innate potential. Self-transcendence is an extension of self-actualization, where people carry their potential beyond themselves to self-fulfillment, which emerges in companionship with others and ultimately a higher state of being that some call God (Maddi, 1996).

In his studies, Maslow (1970) found that people with a strong sense of self-transcendence regularly experience a balance of three types of events—peak experiences, nadir experiences, and plateau experiences. Peak experiences are brief, intense, and shocking events. Nadir experiences involve psychological trauma and near-death experiences. Plateau experiences are relatively serene events that provide people with a sense of enjoyment and happiness. Maslow also found that the important thing in all three types of experiences is that people develop insights and reflections around these experiences that promote a self-transcendent view of life. He developed a hierarchy of needs that people must meet before they can expect to experience self-transcendence (figure 3.2).

Maslow's theory offers a unique perspective for understanding volunteerism. Although it is important to view volunteerism as a complex phenomenon, according to this perspective, volunteerism may simply be an activity that allows people to experience self-actualization and self-transcendence. Volunteerism provides people with opportunities to experience dignity, justice, meaning, mastery, and love for others. Volunteerism also provides people with opportunities to experience a balance of peak, nadir, and plateau experiences. Furthermore, Maslow's theory suggests two roles for social work with people volunteering. First, social workers can

Figure 3.2 Maslow's hierarchy of human needs

Physiological needs	Hunger, thirst, sex
Safety needs	Avoidance of pain and anxiety; security
Belonging needs	Affection, intimacy
Esteem needs	Self-respect, adequacy, efficacy
Self-actualization	Beauty, creativity, justice
Self-transcendence	Altruism, communal consciousness

assist volunteers to make sure their physical and safety needs are met. Second, social workers can help volunteers reflect on their experiences and develop self-transcendent insights.

The two roles derived from Maslow's theory are key strategies for recruiting and retaining committed volunteers. In Duane Wellington's case, there are probably a number of people at his church who would like to volunteer for the mission trip but cannot afford the financial expenses. Duane will have a larger pool of potential volunteers if he works with the pastor to set aside or raise enough funds to cover the expenses. In the same way, Ava Harrington may recruit more mentors if she works with her agency to offer child care to volunteers who are mothers. If she is creative, offering child care does not have to be very expensive. If her agency provides the space, Ava can develop a rotating schedule for the volunteers to share in the child care responsibilities. Sharing the child care responsibilities also provides an opportunity for volunteers to interact with each other, another important component of developing volunteer commitment.

Ava, Raymond, and Duane should also plan volunteer opportunities in such a way that there is enough time for preparation and reflection. Ava and Raymond should facilitate ongoing support groups that meet at different times and on different days during the week for volunteers at their respective agencies. More importantly, however, they should allow enough time in their work schedules for informal conversations with volunteers during which they can use their clinical skills to ask thought-provoking questions and offer reflective feedback. Because they will be developing committed volunteers, the more time Ava and Raymond spend talking with volunteers and meeting their physical and safety needs, the less time they will have to spend looking for replacements.

USING A MULTIDIMENSIONAL APPROACH

Each of the eight human behavior theories offers a different approach to practice with volunteers. Any one view is too narrow to help social workers make sense of the various situations they will encounter when working with volunteers. Instead, a multidimensional approach allows social workers to examine situations from a variety of dimensions. The theories will not be equally useful in all situations. Nevertheless, each perspective will be useful in some situations, and each theory

Table 3.1 Application of human behavior theories to volunteerism

Human Behavior Theory	Specific Elements	Application to Volunteerism
Systems theory and ecological perspective	Goodness of fit	Promotes reciprocal transactions and greater diversity of inputs and outputs
Conflict theory	Power Surplus value Subjection	Volunteering allows people with access to different amounts and types of power to interact for common purposes, produces surplus value, and can be used to deter or contribute to subjection.
Empowerment theory	Collective action Raising critical consciousness	Volunteering promotes individual storytelling, awareness, and eventually critical consciousness and offers potential for collective action.
Phenomenological theory	Uniqueness of social context	People from different cultures and in different locations volunteer in many different settings.
Social learning theory	Modeling and imitation Self-efficacy	Friends, family, and coworkers create an expectation for others to volunteer. As people volunteer in one setting, they gain confidence to take work in new ways
Life span theory and life course theory	Development trajectories Transitions Life events	Volunteering can improve predictable life transitions at all stages of development and lead to significant life events that can change life trajectories for individuals and organizations.
Social exchange theory	Rewards and costs Reciprocal exchanges	There are many potential benefits volunteering. Commitment occurs as individual and group interests merge through reciprocal exchanges.
Maslow's theory of self-actualization and self-transcendence	Hierarchy of needs Peak, nadir, plateau Experiences	Accounting for lower needs can improve recruitment. Opportunities for integrating key experiences for self-transcendence.

should be thought of as an important tool for social work with volunteers. As Gambrill (1990) suggests, social workers need to consider multiple theoretical perspectives so they have adequate information to make decisions about practice situations without drawing exclusively on predisposed biases. Gambrill's point is especially relevant to social work with volunteers because so many factors influence why people begin and continue volunteering. Social workers should draw on the different theories from a strengths perspective by appreciating all the different reasons people volunteer and encouraging individual growth and capacity as they partner with volunteers to address community social problems. Table 3.1 provides a quick reference to the eight theories as they apply to volunteerism.

SUMMARY

Human behavior theories offer different perspectives for explaining and guiding observations of human behavior. Although each theory alone is too narrow to explain the complex phenomenon of volunteerism, a multidimensional framework provides a variety of perspectives to inform social work practice with volunteers. As we turn to the subject of Jane Addams in the next chapter, think about how these theories might help us understand her success in recruiting and working with volunteers.

DISCUSSION QUESTIONS AND LEARNING EXERCISES

1. Think about a nonprofit human services agency in your community that uses volunteers. Do you think the volunteers produce surplus value? Explain your answer.
2. This chapter suggests that volunteer commitment develops from reciprocal exchanges as individual rewards and costs merge with the rewards and costs of organizations. Do you agree? Explain your answer. Can you discuss the process of developing volunteer commitment with another human behavior theory?
3. Interview two different people volunteering with the same organization. Ask them how they became volunteers. Also ask them if and how volunteering has influenced their lives. Try to identify key life events and changes in life trajectories in their stories.
4. Visit two organizations that use volunteers. Describe the unique context of each organization. How does the unique setting influence the experiences of volunteers at each organization? Describe things that each organization can do to enhance the goodness of fit for more volunteers.
5. Think of someone who volunteers. Use each of the theories to describe his or her experiences. Which theories seem most useful? Why? Try thinking of another person whose volunteerism could be best explained with the theories that were not as useful.

Part II

The Relationship between Social Work and Volunteerism

4

Jane Addams: Social Worker and Volunteer

ALONG WITH MARY RICHMOND, JANE ADDAMS IS RECOGNIZED AS ONE OF the matriarchs of the social work profession. Whereas Richmond is normally thought of as a pioneer of the Charity Organization Societies—a precursor to casework and direct practice—social workers associate Addams with Hull-House and the settlement house movement—a precursor to community and organizational practice. The focus of Addams's work, however, went beyond the settlement house movement to an array of issues connected to social and economic justice, including child labor, sanitation, parks and recreation, juvenile justice, world hunger, and women's right to vote.

Addams is one of the most written-about figures in social work, and there are a number of social work textbooks and biographies that highlight her accomplishments and provide useful analyses of her life and personality. Unlike other texts, this chapter does not focus on the person of Jane Addams and her accomplishments; instead, it examines *how* Addams accomplished so much. The chapter posits the following thesis regarding her approach and her accomplishments: Jane Addams's approach to social work practice was to strategically engage the most people possible as potential volunteers to partner with her in addressing social issues. What made her so effective was her ability to recruit, join, and partner with all types of volunteers. Furthermore, she used a pattern of four overlapping strategies in all her work: develop a diverse network of individual relationships, create opportunities to bring people together for any reason, be willing to become a volunteer, and raise critical awareness and guide toward social action.

This chapter presents each strategy in more depth and concludes with examples of how Addams used the same pattern in her social work practice.

DEVELOP A DIVERSE NETWORK OF INDIVIDUAL RELATIONSHIPS

The central element of Jane Addams's accomplishments was her ability to develop genuine relationships with all sorts of different people. Raised in an affluent home, she had relationships with people with access to power and resources. At the same time, she developed genuine relationships with immigrants and laborers. All her relationships were characterized by an enlightened view of people. Addams recognized and embraced the charitable motivations of all people wanting to address poverty. Instead of entering into debate in an effort to persuade others that her way of promoting social and economic justice was the best way, she accepted differing views and found reasons to engage in reciprocal partnerships.

Her view of business professionals and entrepreneurs, in particular, is especially relevant. Addams argued that social workers and business professionals needed each other. She realized that until social workers and business professionals embraced each other and worked together, neither could make a significant contribution to the alleviation of poverty. As a social worker, Addams's approach to business professionals was to appreciate their charitable impulses and desires, see her role as providing business people with direction to channel their charitable desires, and frame the promotion of social and economic justice as corresponding with the goals of capitalism.

Appreciate Charitable Impulses

Addams believed that everyone develops a need or a desire to be useful to society. She posited that men and women need more from life than wealth or the experiences that wealth provides. Perhaps building on her own experiences, she was especially in tune with young men and women whose affluence gave them access to formal education and training. She believed that as young men and women train in philosophy, the humanities, the arts, business, and science, they develop ideals and passions for contributing to humanity. Addams (1892) stated, "They feel a fatal want of harmony between theory and action" (p. 6).

As they transition into the real world, however, the realities of developing a family, their desire for material possessions, and their efforts to pursue careers consume the majority of their energies. As a result, their ideals and passions remain dormant or become repressed. However, Addams expected that at some point in the future, these young men and women would become dissatisfied with life and want more in terms of purpose. She added: "I think it is hard for us to realize how seriously many of them are taking the notion of human brotherhood, how eagerly they long to give tangible expression to the democratic ideal. . . . There is a heritage of noble obligation which young people accept and long to perpetuate. The desire for action, the wish to right wrong and alleviate suffering, haunts them daily" (Addams, 1892, p. 6). Addams expressed great empathy for these young men and women because she believed their unfulfilled need to help others resulted in feelings of atrophy that left them disconnected from their communities. As a social worker, she saw her role as helping them find ways of being useful to people in need.

Provide Direction for Charitable Pursuits

As much as Hull-House provided services and advocated for the poor, Addams made clear that the settlement house movement also provided people with opportunities for service. She believed advocacy and progress occurred when a community's interests represented the interests of all types of men and women. Although the settlement house was located in a poor working-class neighborhood, she made sure that the programs and events attracted people from different social strata. Gatherings to discuss art, music, science, homemaking, and political issues allowed Addams to attract educated and affluent people to the programs. Once people became regular attendees, she would invite them to go a step further and volunteer. In the same way, as local people benefited from the support and services offered, Addams would find ways for them to volunteer to support the functioning of the house and become active in addressing social problems in the community.

Align Social and Economic Justice with Capitalism

Along with appreciating all people and providing direction for them to act upon their charitable impulses, Addams carefully framed issues of social and economic justice within the context of capitalism. Although she clearly sought to eliminate poverty, she embraced democracy and the capitalist market economy. Instead of ostracizing people motivated by profit and wealth, she embraced them and found ways to communicate why they should care about justice. In fact, Addams did not see the pursuits of wealth and justice as incompatible; rather her social work practice was predicated on her philosophy that democracy and self-interest were enhanced when there was at least a minimum standard of living as well as civil and social participation by all people. For example, her work with trade unions and her successful efforts to reform child labor laws were based on the premise that people must develop as cultivated members of society with a consciousness for both industry and justice. As an advocate, she preferred quiet and orderly expression over more aggressive tactics. She framed the welfare of the poor and laborers as a part of the creation of a stable market economy and the ideal democratic state (Addams, 1897).

CREATE OPPORTUNITIES TO BRING PEOPLE TOGETHER FOR ANY REASON

If developing an extensive network of friends and colleagues was the essential element of Addams's accomplishments, then creating reasons to bring them together was her primary practice method. From the beginning, Hull-House served as a meeting place where Addams brought people in contact with one another. She called the meetings social clubs.

The social club was the vehicle for every aspect of Addams's work and accomplishments. In essence, a social club was a gathering of volunteers who came together for any purpose. Addams belonged to and organized all types of clubs, including home economics clubs, science clubs, literature clubs, recreation clubs, athletic clubs, debate clubs, and clubs for women and for men. Whatever the topic, all the clubs shared the same three purposes: to provide opportunities for self-improvement, opportunities for "clean" recreation, and a platform for community action and participation.

Opportunities for Self-Improvement

First, the clubs focused on providing opportunities for self-improvement. The residents at Hull-House and the surrounding areas tended to work long hours in factories, doing tedious and repetitive tasks. Addams was concerned for the welfare of the community and the workers. She believed that factory work left people disengaged from the happenings in the community. As people became acculturated to their daily work routines, they did not have the time or energy to fulfill their civic responsibilities. As social problems such as adverse living conditions, juvenile delinquency, alcoholism, and poverty escalated, Addams feared residents would become apathetic. She thought people needed access to social and intellectual events to enhance their lives. By providing stimulating meetings, Addams made sure that people had constructive activities to anticipate during their days in the factories. Likewise, the clubs provided their children with a chance to expand their interests. Many of the children went on to become doctors, lawyers, scholars, and teachers instead of becoming a second generation of factory workers (Addams, 1910b).

Opportunities for "Clean" Recreation

In addition to providing opportunities for self-improvement, Addams viewed the clubs as an alternative to less enriching activities. She believed the residents living on the West Side of Chicago were susceptible to corrupt, shady, and immoral types of recreation. Her fear, and the reality of the community environment, was that bars, nightclubs, prostitution, and gambling were becoming more prevalent in that part of the city. She explained, "Many people living there are very poor, the majority of them without leisure or energy for anything. . . . Too often their only place of meeting is a saloon, their only host a bartender" (Addams, 1910b, p. 255). She was especially concerned for younger people, for whom safe environments for entertainment were scarce and the lack of which was becoming a social problem:

> Such young people, well meaning but impatient of control, become the easy victims of the worst type of public dance halls and of even darker places, whose purposes are hidden under music and dancing. We were thoroughly frightened when we learned that during the year which ended last December, more than twenty-five thousand young people under the age of twenty-five passed through the Juvenile and Municipal Courts of Chicago—approximately one out of every eighty of the entire population, or one out of fifty-two of those under twenty-five years of age. One's heart aches for these young people caught by the outside glitter of city gaiety, who make such a fervent attempt to snatch it for themselves. (Addams, 1910b, p. 244)

Her solution was to use the social clubs to provide opportunities for "clean" recreation. She set out to host gatherings that offered opportunities for young people to have fun, were safe, and set a high standard of decorum. The clubs planned parties, picnics, dances, and festivals to which people of different age groups were always invited. Addams posited that including different age groups was vital to setting high standards because parents could feel safe about their children attending activities and it gave older adults the important role of sharing their experienced wisdom in planning the events and taught young people to associate having fun with spending time with adults.

Platform for Community Action

Whatever the specific topic or event, Addams used the clubs as a platform for community action and participation. Although organizing a literature club or a gardening club may seem irrelevant to social work practice, Addams saw beyond the topics that attracted participants and focused on the process of what happens when a group of people gather for any purpose. The key purpose of the clubs was to create opportunities for what she called "social intercourse" among people of different nationalities, beliefs, and interests. Addams (1917) shared the importance of social intercourse in her address to the Woman's City Club of Chicago: "People must have an interest and desire for cooperation with a great many other people, but they cannot get that interest and cooperation unless there is an understanding of their needs with the sense of obligation and fellowship, which can only come if cultivated with opportunities to gather" (p. 3). The clubs represented a method for cultivating a sense of obligation and fellowship among people. She described the clubs as providing people with the means to produce the sort of energy and understanding needed to address social problems. To Addams (1910a), social intercourse could bring about a "genuine sense of participation, and a public spirit" that could do good (p. 43).

Addams believed that in any social club two things occur that can lead people to become more informed and engaged in the community. First, group participation sensitizes people to tune in to the happenings of other people in the club. Second, as people engage in activities in a social club, they become mobilized for further action and participation in other areas. She described it as a simple process.

When neighbors of Hull-House participated in the clubs with people from other parts of Chicago, they developed relationships based upon similar interests. These were people with vastly different religions, languages, traditions, and family backgrounds who established genuine companionship with one another. Eventually, the relationships spilled over to other areas of life and club members made genuine efforts to connect with each other. As friends, they shared stories of daily struggles that could eventually become full-blown social problems. Because the club members were already used to working together, it was then easy for them to shift the direction of their activities toward actions specifically focused on addressing social problems. Addams (1910b) explained, "The value of social clubs broadens out in one's mind to an instrument of companionship through which many may be led from a sense of isolation to one of civic responsibility" (p. 253).

BE WILLING TO BECOME A VOLUNTEER

Her relationships and the voluntary social clubs she organized are not enough to explain how Addams managed to attract enough committed people to sustain the clubs' operations for so many years (in some cases as long as forty years). Chapter 2 presented several reasons people begin and continue volunteering. Sustained membership in these voluntary social clubs was probably linked to the quality of communication, the training and emotional support members received, group cohesiveness, the convenience of meeting times and schedules, and the sense of efficacy members got from participating. If Addams had just brought people together, the development of the clubs would have been simply the outcome of chance. Moreover, she might have wasted an enormous amount of time and energy. If the right mix of people gathered, then a club would emerge and continue. If the wrong mix of people gathered, then there would be no additional meetings. Given all she accomplished, there must be another explanation for the longevity of the clubs.

There are actually two reasons. First, Addams did more than organize the clubs: she participated as a member. Second, as a member, she educated others about social problems and mobilized them to take action. Just as Addams was willing to live side by side with the poor, she placed herself on equal footing with other volunteers. She recognized that as an individual, her efforts to advocate social and economic justice were useless: "The word of a single individual is too feeble to overcome inertia" (Addams, 1898, p. 552). Therefore, she positioned herself in the ranks of volunteers as a member in different clubs and associations.

Although she may not have been consciously aware of the specific reasons people begin and continue volunteering, her willingness to participate put her in position to promote sustained membership. Her deliberate position as a member and organizer allowed her to be in touch with other participants, on one hand, and to orchestrate the direction of the clubs, on the other hand. As a member, Addams could personally assess the amount and quality of communication among participants, she could gauge the level of group camaraderie, and she could provide and receive support. As both a member and an organizer, she could plan meetings at the most convenient times and encourage the club to sponsor activities that would give members a sense of accomplishment. She would eventually take on leadership positions, although only after she had earned credibility as a member. In nearly every one of her voluntary associations, she used her communication skills to raise critical awareness about social problems throughout the group's membership.

RAISE CRITICAL AWARENESS AND GUIDE TOWARD SOCIAL ACTION

As a member of volunteer groups within and outside Hull-House, Addams often guided the discussion and the focus of the groups toward community action. As Addams participated as a member in voluntary social clubs, she became a natural part of group interactions. Then, when a pressing social issue emerged, she brought it to the attention of her fellow members. In some circumstances, she directed the discussions during the course of ordinary conversations. In other instances, she formally addressed the clubs. In addition, she was often invited to speak to clubs to which she did not belong. Therefore, most of her work was done either in her capacity as a volunteer member of a social club or as someone addressing a group of volunteers.

It is important to note that Addams's four strategies were not always used in a particular order. Sometimes Addams developed a genuine friendship with a person who invited her to talk to a group. In some cases, she would later become a member of the group. Other times, she developed relationships in a group that she helped organize. When she developed relationships, it was easier for her to encourage the group to spend time on activities geared toward community action. The following section offers examples of how she used the four strategies to raise critical awareness and guide people toward action.

The Development of Hull-House

The development of Hull-House is usually portrayed in social work textbooks as the sole work of Jane Addams (e.g., Morales & Sheafor, 2004; Zastrow, 2004). While she should be credited as a skilled social worker for being its visionary and the catalyst, Hull-House would have never been established if she had worked alone. Moreover, the house would never have remained in operation for over four decades. A closer look behind how Hull-House was developed demonstrates the central role of her partnerships with volunteers.

From the beginning, Addams worked with her close friend Ellen Starr to establish Hull-House. At first Addams did not even want to move to Chicago. She was living with Mary Blaisdell, a close friend and former teacher, in Cedarville, Illinois, where she helped care for Mary and her child, who were both ill. However, she and Ellen had discussed their plans to settle in a poor section of Chicago for at least two years. In 1889 Ellen finally persuaded her to leave Mary and join her.

Once in Chicago, Addams put herself in situations that would allow her to develop a network of personal relationships. She started attending a large and prestigious church and went to Bible studies as much as possible. As she became a regular attendee at Fourth Presbyterian Church, she had opportunities to develop relationships with the pastoral staff as well as other people attending the church. A few of the people with whom she developed relationships were active volunteers doing social service work in the city. Remember that religious congregations are a specific type of volunteer association. Moreover, the various groups that met for Bible studies represented smaller volunteer groups that were part of a network of groups that operated under the auspices of the larger congregation.

In the context of her personal relationships, Addams would share her vision for a place in the neighborhood where people could live and gather together to develop a heightened sense of community. Her friends would then invite her to share her plan with groups of people with whom they were connected. She was invited to speak to the leaders of the Clybourn Avenue Mission, the Armour Mission, the Chicago Ethical Cultural Society, Plymouth Congregational Church, and Central Church. Many of the people in attendance at the meetings were very wealthy. Addams often received an enthusiastic response and offers of assistance. Eventually, she gained support from some of the most powerful religious, philanthropic, and business figures in the city. It is important to note that when she was invited to speak, the invitation was always coordinated by friends from church who were somehow connected to these other groups. Therefore, when she was invited to speak to a group, it was in her capacity as a member of Fourth Presbyterian Church and the friend of a member of the other group. Although her communication skills and vision were often the cause of the positive response she received, her church membership and friendships gave her instant credibility as someone to whom it was worth paying attention.

A friend from church arranged for Addams to present her plans to the Woman's City Club of Chicago. She made such a positive impression on the club's members that they pledged their support and invited her to apply for membership in the club. An invitation to become a member was rare, as the club usually only accepted one new member a year. However, because her friend from church was one of the most influential members of the club, Addams's application for membership was accepted.

As a volunteer member of the Woman's City Club of Chicago, she turned an old and battered building into Hull-House. Stated differently, as a volunteer member of Fourth Presbyterian Church, she developed relationships with people who listened to her ideas and connected her to other volunteer groups, including the Woman's City Club of Chicago, of which she became a member and gained the support of a number of powerful people who helped her create Hull-House. Shortly thereafter, Addams created a sister club called the Hull-House Woman's Club that would eventually become one of the largest women's volunteer clubs in the city of Chicago.

Sanitation

The Hull-House Woman's Club emerged after Addams developed a relationship with Jenny Dow Harvey, a kindergarten teacher living with her at the house. The club was initially started as a place where mothers in the neighborhood could gather to support one another. During the club's first year, the meetings focused on providing the mothers with companionship and allowing them to exchange helpful homemaking tips and parenting strategies. Eventually, however, Addams guided the discussions of the club toward the social problems associated with the poor sanitation on the West Side of Chicago. She expressed her concern that the rising death rates in the Nineteenth Ward might have something to do with the handling of garbage in their neighborhoods. Knowing that many of the women worked as domestic servants and, after a long day of work, had to come home to take care of their children, she framed the issue as one relevant to mothers interested in protecting the safety and well-being of their children (Addams, 1910b).

After several meetings devoted to the subject of sanitation, a number of the club members decided to make a formal assessment of how garbage and waste were being handled in their part of the city. The plan involved reviewing city ordinances, monitoring the removal of trash, and spending three evenings each week examining all the back roads and alleyways located on the West Side of Chicago. Within six months, the women discovered and substantiated evidence of over a thousand violations of the law that were supposed to be documented by city inspectors. Since the women found no official record of the violations, Addams mailed a report documenting all the violations to the Chicago health department. As a result, the three city inspectors assigned to the West Side of Chicago were transferred due to unsatisfactory service.

While the club's efforts led to the transfer of the city inspectors, it did not lead to any immediate improvements in sanitation. Improvements occurred only after the women of the club supported Addams once she was appointed garbage inspector for the Nineteenth Ward by the mayor. Several of the women took turns helping Addams by getting up early in the morning to make sure the men hired to collect the garbage were on time. Other club members periodically followed the garbage wagons to make sure trash was being discarded in the right place. Still others continued examining back roads and alleys to make sure each building had the proper number of garbage receptacles. A few club members even helped Addams set up a couple of garbage incinerators, which allowed her to cut the amount—and costs— of trash being transported to the dumps. She was also able to negotiate an agreement with a local factory to purchase destroyed tin cans (Addams, 1910b). The factory used the cans to produce small weights used to balance windows.

Four years after Addams and the Hull-House Woman's Club began examining how trash collection was handled, the neighborhood looked much different. There was great improvement in the cleanliness and comfort in the area. More importantly, the death rate in the area dropped significantly, making the Nineteenth Ward a much safer place to raise children. When the good news was shared at a club meeting, Addams attributed the loud applause from the membership to a "genuine sense of participation in the result" (Addams, 1910b, p. 205).

Child Labor and Recreation

Child labor emerged as an issue for Addams in much the same way as sanitation. In addition to the Hull-House Woman's Club, Addams organized separate volunteer social clubs for men and for children. During Hull-House's first year, she was invited to attend a boy's science club. At the meeting, she learned of three boys who had been injured at a neighborhood factory. Apparently the boys were working with a machine that was missing a safety guard needed for proper operation. After one of the injured boys died, Addams went to the factory, expecting the owners to share in her horror and remorse and purchase safety guards for the machines to prevent injuries in the future. To her surprise, they did nothing. As she had done with sanitation, Addams brought the issue to the woman's club and gathered support from several members to begin an in-depth assessment.

During the next several months, the women made visits to businesses in the neighborhood, documenting any work practices they deemed potentially dangerous or unfitting for children. They found children performing all sorts of monotonous factory work. For instance, they saw four-year-old children sitting on stools for eight hours at a time, helping women make garments in sweatshops. They also found young children walking outside all day in the middle of winter in Chicago selling newspapers. In addition, they watched thirteen-and-fourteen-year-olds work ten-hour days pasting labels on boxes and rotating laundered sheets and towels at a commercial laundry facility. They also interviewed the parents of at least two other children who died from accidents related to their work (Addams, 1910b).

After the women completed their assessment, Addams and Florence Kelley, another volunteer member of the woman's club, brought their findings to the Illinois State Bureau of Labor. As a result of their assessment, the bureau made a special report to the Illinois legislature. In the report, the bureau recommended establishing the state's first factory law to regulate working conditions and set a minimum age at which children could legally work. The legislature agreed with the report and drafted a bill for consideration (Davis, 2000).

Between the time the bill was drafted and the child labor law enacted in 1899, Addams, Kelley, and other members of the Hull-House Woman's Club worked tirelessly to gain support from different groups of people in the community. They spoke at a variety of volunteer groups such as trade unions, benefit societies, church organizations, and social clubs. In addition, they made sure to frame the issue of child labor in a context that made sense to their audiences. For example, when talking to trade and labor unions, they framed the issue within the context of wages. They explained that as working men trying to earn enough money to provide for their families, they should support the passage of child labor legislation to limit the supply of labor and protect their wages. On the other hand, when talking to a group of mothers, they discussed how children have physical and emotional needs that monotonous factory work does not fulfill. They need proper education and time to just develop, play, and grow without the burden of helping to support their families (Addams, 1899).

As Addams campaigned for regulation of child labor, she recognized that the issue could not be addressed as a stand-alone social problem. If children in the neighborhood weren't at work, they would have to be somewhere. Therefore, along with sponsoring and supporting child labor legislation, she worked with other volunteers to establish a nursery, a kindergarten, and a playground in the community. She also advocated creating community parks and recreation. To Addams, access to recreation in the community was a vital means of promoting greater participation in activity that could lead to social and political progress. She argued that in addition to regulating labor and providing education, local and state government needed to be involved in the creation of parks and opportunities for recreation (Addams, 1911).

Women's Movement

Addams's participation in the women's movement was different from the previous examples. Whereas the other examples illustrate how Addams used the four strategies toward specific ends, the rights and the roles and participation in society of women was an enduring cause that shaped nearly everything she did. Addams's role in the women's movement highlights the emphasis she placed on the use of volunteer clubs for moving women's issues forward and her belief in the use of the same methods for other social issues, such as world hunger. Moreover, it is within the context of her work in the movement that Addams provided the most succinct description of the process by which individuals are brought together and, over time, become active and sustained volunteers.

For Addams, the role and participation of women in society was an underlying current that helped lead to the creation of Hull-House. As much as Hull-House was designed to help the poor, Addams also created the settlement house to provide herself and other women with a place to meet, organize, and expand their interests beyond paternally defined roles for women. During the early years at Hull-House, organizing a voluntary club for women to study literature, poetry, philosophy, and science was truly progressive.

As she participated in the clubs, she would also discuss the need for women to expand their influence in political and social issues. Demonstrating her ability to assess each individual context, she did not focus her discussions specifically on obtaining equal rights for women. Instead, she strategically framed her discussions around the topic of women's obligations to fulfill their roles as the nurturers and caretakers of society. Her strategy is most noticeable in her efforts to address world hunger and promote women's right to vote. As she advocated women's right to vote, she did not frame the issue as a matter of women's equality (although a good reason in and of itself, but probably not as productive for the given context) but as an extension of their homemaking responsibilities. She stated: "Women today are failing to discharge their duties to their own households properly simply because they do not perceive that as society grows more complicated it is necessary that women shall extend their sense of responsibility to many things outside of their own homes if they would continue to preserve the home in its entirety" (Addams, 1910c, p. 21).

Addams's appeal to women's obligations continued as she advocated their participation in the fight against world hunger. From 1890 to 1917, women's clubs from all over the country developed and joined together to form a national volunteer organization called the General Federation of Women's Clubs. As the membership grew, Addams was outspoken about their potential to affect world hunger. With the General Federation of Women's Clubs established, she challenged the organization's worth to society if the membership could not rally to address the food shortage crisis. She again called upon women's "traditional relation to food and her obligation to nurture the world" (Addams, 1918, p. 252). In contrast to men, whom she said reduced the issue of international food supply to a commercial and political leveraging tool for foreign affairs, Addams posited that an organized effort by volunteer women could focus on the daily human need for nutritious food. Moreover, she believed that, if successful, their methods for addressing international affairs could set a precedent by which large government systems could enter into voluntary associations with one another with a platform built upon similar interests, tolerance for diversity, and well-being for all (Addams, 1922).

Analyzing the women's movement in its entirety, Addams described the process by which individuals are brought together and, over time, develop into active and sustained volunteers. She acknowledged that most of the civic triumphs were the result of the volunteer clubs involved in the women's movement. She described the importance of the early years, when club members discussed common interests. She stated that it was easy for others to "treat lightly this period of club development" (Addams, 1930, p. 94). However, she believed that as the women interacted in discussing common interests, they would develop an interest in civic affairs as issues came to their attention. For Addams, it was not difficult to take a group that was debating the protagonist in a novel or the theme of a piece of art and from that develop the group's interest in making sure public schools had access to books and building picturesque parks so children could develop their creative abilities. As the purpose of club meetings evolved from abstract study to direct civic action, natural opportunities for women to engage in shaping public opinion and reforming local and state policy arose. As women gained experience and a sense of efficacy from successfully participating in civic reform, the clubs became ready to "investigate any civic situation which seemed to call for vigorous action" (Addams, 1930, p. 99).

SUMMARY

This chapter looked at the methods behind the accomplishments of Jane Addams. Addams was a wonderful speaker, a great writer, and an intelligent, persistent, and insightful woman. She was the catalyst or key participant in many social welfare endeavors that would never have happened if she had not been personally involved. At the same time, Addams would not have accomplished anything without the active and sustained support of other people.

Beginning with her earliest work, she recognized how important it was to enlist supporters. The methods she used are what made her so effective. Her primary asset was her appreciation for diversity, as she viewed all people as potential volunteers. As such, she was willing to work with anyone who could help her advance a social cause or activity. Her view of people allowed her to develop a vast network of genuine relationships, bring people together, and encourage them to participate as actual volunteers. Then, as she gained credibility, she waited for the right moments to raise critical awareness and move groups toward taking action. In essence, Addams was so successful because she herself was willing to be a volunteer and partner with volunteers. However, as the next chapter will show, social workers have not always been able to follow Addams's example and engage with volunteers, and as a result, the profession's relationship with volunteerism has suffered.

DISCUSSION QUESTIONS AND LEARNING EXERCISES

1. This chapter suggests that what made Jane Addams so effective was her ability to partner with volunteers. Do you agree? Explain your answer.
2. One of Jane Addams's key strategies was her willingness to become a volunteer. Is spending time participating in volunteer groups a part of effective social work practice today? Explain your answer.
3. What volunteer opportunities would make you more effective in your particular area of practice? For instance, it may be useful for a social worker practicing as a mental health case manager or clinician to be an active member at the local chapter of the National Alliance on Mental Illness.
4. Jane Addams created opportunities to bring people together for social intercourse. Conduct a social intercourse assessment of your community. Examine the opportunities available to bring people together. Now think of all the stakeholders influencing your agency. Where do they gather? Assess whether or not there are social workers at these gatherings.

5

Social Work's Historical Relationship to Volunteerism

ALTHOUGH SOCIAL WORK RECOGNIZES JANE ADDAMS AS ONE OF THE matriarchs of the profession, current practice looks entirely different from what she envisioned. As practice settings have become more diverse (hospitals, mental health centers, corporations, drug and alcohol treatment centers, hospices, etc.), the basic construct of social work practice has narrowed. Instead of using social work knowledge, values, and skills to partner with people to address systemic social problems, the majority of social work practice involves individuals providing treatment and services to individual clients. Social work practice methods that involve partnering with volunteers are almost nonexistent.

This chapter examines what happened to the relationship between social work and volunteerism. It seeks to answer the question, How did the social work profession, which owes its existence to the efforts of volunteers, lose touch with volunteerism as a central means of delivering effective services and advocating social and economic justice? After describing the historical relationship between social work and volunteerism, the chapter examines two reasons—insecurity and avoidance—to explain that relationship.

THE HISTORICAL RELATIONSHIP

The historical relationship between social work and volunteerism can be divided into three discernable periods. Before we discuss the three periods, it's important to begin with a brief review of the underlying importance of volunteerism to American society.

Volunteerism is crucial to American society. More specifically, having the freedom to organize and participate in volunteer associations is vital to a functioning democracy. The more citizens involve themselves as volunteers, the closer they come to making the ideals of democracy a reality (Ellis & Noyes, 1990). In 1835, when Alex de Tocqueville visited the United States to study American democracy, he observed that the key that enabled the Americans to make democracy work was their disposition toward forming volunteer associations. Tocqueville (1835) commented on this unique aspect of American society: "Americans of all ages, all stations in life and all types of dispositions are forever forming [volunteer] associations. They are not only commercial and industrial associations in which they take part, but others of a thousand types—religion, moral, serious, futile, very general and very limited, immensely large and very minute" (p. 485).

The propensity for forming volunteer associations in America began as an effort for survival. In the seventeenth century, cooperative farm ventures were formed to assist with building construction, collective cattle herding, and labor sharing (Barck & Lefler, 1958; Earle, 1923). Groups of volunteers would also work together to erect churches that would function both as places of worship and as meeting places for all types of community functions (Rines, 1936). Government took the form of voluntary town meetings where unpaid officials were selected to fulfill numerous roles such as clerks of the market, town criers, and surveyors of the highways. Although at first volunteer efforts did not formally address organized charity, as the population increased, benevolent societies formed to provide relief to the poor when families were unavailable to assist them. As these benevolent societies failed to meet the growing needs of the poor, they eventually began to regard the entire community as ultimately responsible for the care of the unfortunate (Fairlie, 1920). It was through the formation of volunteer associations, therefore, that the need for community social welfare was recognized.

During the eighteenth and nineteenth centuries, nearly every advance in American society came about as a result of volunteerism (Berger & Neuhaus, 1977; Ellis & Noyes, 1990). Volunteer societies formed to improve transportation, sanitation, communication, fire prevention, public safety, and education. Volunteer associations also advocated fair labor practices, especially concerning children; women's rights; African Americans' rights; better medical practices; and humane treatment of the mentally ill and brought attention to the debilitating effects of alcohol (Carter, 1926; Cubberly, 1944; Dunlop, 1965; Laidler, 1968). Ellis and Noyes (1990) even go so far as to suggest that nearly every social need recognized and addressed by the government was first recognized and advocated for by some volunteer effort.

Even the social reform advances of the Progressive Era depended upon the volunteer collaboration between the lower and middle classes (Hofstadter, 1963). Whereas their efforts had once been fueled by a need for survival, now the common thread of their collaboration was humanitarianism. During the Progressive Era, volunteer efforts worked toward encouraging the government to act "upon the public's civic alertness and will" (Ellis & Noyes, 1990, p. 168) and to temper the zealousness for economic prosperity with the protection of human rights. As the chapter will show, however, reformers did not intend for increased professional and government involvement to replace the participation or responsibility of volunteers.

Volunteerism: The Origin of Social Work

Simply stated, the profession of social work owes its existence to volunteerism. Volunteers founded relief societies, children's homes, day care programs, recreation services, family and child welfare associations, and mental health associations. In other words, volunteers preceded social work in almost every field of practice (Anderson & Ambrosino, 1992). Many introductory texts on social work and social welfare recognize the profession's origin in volunteerism. For example, Morales and Sheafor (2004) describe the beginning of social work as being "found in the extensive volunteer movement during the formative years of the United States" (p. 40). Most notably, the contributions of volunteers are recognized as essential to the development of the Charity Organization Society (COS) movement and the settlement house movement (see, e.g., Ellis & Noyes 1990). It is in these two movements that the role of volunteerism is linked to the emergence of the social work profession.

As a volunteer movement, the COS movement emerged to become a significant precursor to social work, representing the first efforts to serve poor people in a systematic way. Essentially the movement consisted of volunteers who assisted families in meeting their physical, economic, emotional, and spiritual needs. In 1877 the Reverend S. Humphrey Gurteen established the first COS in Buffalo, New York, to provide an alternative method to indiscriminate giving for helping the poor (Pumphrey & Pumphrey, 1961). The proponents of COS worked to make philanthropic practices more systematic and efficient. The principle method to improve efficiency was volunteer cooperation. COS organizations usually consisted of an executive council of volunteer leaders who were already actively engaged in providing services to the poor. Moreover, the council trained direct service volunteers, commonly referred to as "family visitors," to screen applicants, conduct family histories, and manage cases to make informed choices about the best ways to provide support (Putnam, 1887).

As discussed in chapter 4, the settlement house movement also emerged from the efforts of volunteers. As a volunteer member of the Woman's City Club of Chicago, Jane Addams turned an old and battered building into Hull-House. The Hull-House Woman's Club would become one of the largest women's volunteer clubs in the city of Chicago. Addams (1910b) acknowledged the value of the women's volunteer clubs, saying, "The entire organization of the social life at Hull House, while it has been fostered and directed by residents and others, has been largely pushed and vitalized from within by the club members themselves" (p. 253). More specifically, it was within the context of her membership in these clubs that Addams was able to encourage fellowship among women of different ethnicities, connect residents of Hull-House with better housing, and advocate improved conditions within Chicago's city jails.

Social Work's Attempt to Distinguish Itself

The COS and settlement house movements characterized the shift away from individual and volunteer philanthropy toward scientific charity. As people such as Mary Richmond, Josephine Shaw Lowell, Robert Hunter, and Edward Devine recognized the importance of comprehensive assessments, clear record keeping, and effective coordination of services, there was a growing recognition of the need for people to be professionally trained to work with the poor and needy (Morales &

Sheafor, 2004). Professional training, however, was never intended to replace individual concerns and volunteer efforts. In fact, Mary Richmond (1908) believed that social workers could never completely stand in as the social servants of the community. She believed instead that a basic responsibility of the social work profession was to guide and support the efforts of volunteers.

As the delivery of services became more systematic, however, Richmond's reminder and Addams's example of the importance of reciprocal partnerships between professional helpers and volunteers were quickly forgotten. By the time President Roosevelt's administration enacted the New Deal, the government had become primarily responsible for social welfare services, and social work became the primary profession in the provision of these services (Ellis & Noyes, 1990; Katz, 1996). Trattner (1999) summarizes the shift in the relationship this way:

> The devaluation of volunteers did not take the form of outright rejection, largely because of the long tradition of volunteerism in social welfare and because professional social workers needed the power, influence, and financial help of volunteers. What occurred, then, was a reversal of roles. Whereas earlier what was considered the real work of the agency, friendly visiting, was conducted by volunteers and the menial labor by paid staff members, by the turn of the century, the opposite was beginning to occur; volunteers did the office work or, by serving as trustees helped shape policy and raise funds, while the work in the field, casework, was in the hands of paid professional agents. Viewed earlier as a civic duty, volunteerism became, instead, a privilege granted by agencies to those who accepted their authority and discipline. (p. 103)

Reconciliation in Times of Need

Of course, the social work profession did not abandon ties with volunteerism altogether. Instead, as Trattner (1999) points out, the relationship shifted. Cnaan (1999) accurately depicts the relationship as one in which social workers develop and deliver systematic and professional services while volunteers provide a hidden safety net. Indeed, during certain critical periods, social workers have enlisted the help of volunteers. During the Great Depression and World War II, social workers turned to volunteers as necessary personnel for addressing social needs. In the 1950s, volunteers were partners in auxiliary social work services, helping as fundraisers, educators, office assistants, and drivers. In the 1960s, some volunteers moved into direct service roles, offering lay therapy in child abuse and neglect programs, counseling on telephone crisis lines, advocating in domestic violence programs, and participating in self-help and mutual aid groups (Anderson & Ambrosino, 1992).

More recently, in response to the shortage of professionals available, social work is again turning to volunteers, this time asking them to fill many traditional social work jobs. The idea is that if properly trained and supervised, volunteers can fill in and allow professional social workers to focus on the more complex aspects of practice (O'Neill, 2002).

EXPLAINING WHAT HAPPENED

Reviewing the three periods in the relationship between social work and volunteerism only illustrates the shift that occurred. They do not explain what caused the shift in the relationship. At some point, however, something must have happened to make social work want to separate and distinguish itself from volunteerism. The answer is found in the 1915 proceedings of the forty-second annual session of the National Conference of Charities and Corrections—a precursor to the National Association of Social Workers.

Flexner's Analysis of Social Work

At the 1915 NCCC conference, Abraham Flexner, an accepted authority on the study of professions, was invited to present an analysis of whether social work was a profession. Apparently, the organizers assumed that Flexner's presentation would offer them assurance that social work was, or was about to become, a full-fledged profession similar to medicine, law, and engineering. They were not prepared for the possibility that he would draw the opposite conclusion.

At the beginning of his presentation, Flexner distinguished between the relative use of the term "professional" and the absolute use of the term "profession." To Flexner, the term "professional" loosely denotes a person who devotes his or her time to a specific activity, be it baseball, basketball, dancing, acting, bartending, or truck driving. In contrast, Flexner defined the term "profession" as a limited group of activities that meet a certain predetermined set of objective criteria. He spelled out six criteria that separate a profession from all other occupations. He then used the criteria to assess whether social work was a profession.

1. Professions involve activities that are essentially intellectual—the thinking process is the main instrument applied to address problems. Individuals who use their intelligence in their professional capacity are often held accountable for outcomes. To Flexner (1915) the activities of a social worker were definitely intellectual: "The worker must possess fine powers of analysis and discrimination, breadth and flexibility of sympathy, sound judgment, skill in utilizing whatever resources available, facility in devising new combinations. These operations are assuredly of intellectual quality" (p. 17).
2. Professions derive their own raw material from science and learning—the thinking process uses information specifically learned for the given field instead of drawing upon knowledge and experience that is easily accessible from general sources of information. Flexner indicated that social workers perform a mediating function with material developed by other fields instead of using raw material that they developed themselves. He questioned whether the social worker was a professional or the person who brought professional activity into action. He stated, "The very variety of the situations [a social

worker] encounters compels him to be not a professional agent so much as the mediator invoking this or that professional agency" (Flexner, 1915, p. 17).

3. Professions apply learning in a way that is practical—the thinking process and the development of raw knowledge have a clear-cut end that is recognized and sanctioned by society. To Flexner social work did not have definitive ends that distinguished it from other professions. He viewed social work as being in touch with many professions rather than a profession in and of itself. "It appears not so much a definite field as an aspect of work in many fields" (Flexner, 1915, p. 18).

4. Professions use a transmittable technique that requires education—there are specific objectives a practitioner must master before gaining entry into the profession. In addition, there is an agreed-upon standard for the admission requirements and the content and length of education. Flexner viewed the fields of social work as too numerous and diverse to constitute a single educational discipline. Although he determined schools of social work to be important, he posited that the content was not technically professional. Instead, he characterized the education of social workers as supplemental and "broadly cultural in a variety of realms of civic and social interest" (Flexner, 1915, p. 18).

5. Professions are self-organized—the activities of a profession are so definitive, so absorbing in interest, so richly engaging in duties and responsibilities that individuals and their families tend to organize around a strong nucleus. As Flexner pointed out in his presentation, the annual conferences testified to the development of professional self-identity leading to self-organization.

6. Professions become increasingly altruistic in motivation—as time goes on, devotion to the common well-being of society becomes more and more an accepted mark of professional activities. Eventually the interests of individual practitioners of a given profession yield to the increasing realization of responsibility to the larger social environment. To Flexner, this was the one criterion in which social work exceeds most other occupations. Although he would not officially call social work a profession, he did acknowledge that social work's professional spirit, in many ways, was what mattered most. According to Flexner (1915), "The unselfish devotion of those who have chosen to give themselves to making the world a fitter place to live in can fill social work with the professional spirit and thus to some extent lift it above all the distinctions which I have been at pains to make" (p. 19).

The Sustained Impact of Flexner's Presentation

Flexner described social workers as intelligent, kindhearted, and resourceful people who perform an important mediating function. In his opinion, however, so-

cial work was not a profession. What happened thereafter, and still continues to occur, was an all-out attempt to demonstrate to colleagues, clients, society, and most
importantly ourselves that social work was and is a profession. And if social work
was to be considered a profession, there would have to be separation between the
field of social work and the efforts of volunteerism. Social work thus abandoned its
roots in its quest for professional status.

In the decades following Flexner's presentation, the focus of social work was
dominated by its search for a knowledge base and practice methods. In its search,
social work became infatuated with psychiatry and Freudian psychology, which
conveniently offered two advantages in terms of achieving professional status. First,
the use of psychiatry and Freudian psychology allowed social work to claim adher-
ence to a specific knowledge base that would satisfy the gap pointed out by Flexner.
Within a few years of his presentation, several leading social workers began promoting their new knowledge base. Eventually psychiatric social work emerged as a
distinct field of practice, and Freudian psychology (and the theories derived from
Freudian psychology) emerged as the primary theory in most areas of practice.

Second, psychiatry and Freudian psychology offered social work the opportunity to associate its practice methods with the medical model of practice, thus ele-
vating the status of social workers to that of trained experts providing treatment.
Instead of emphasizing the larger environmental causes of poverty and other community problems, the scope of social work practice narrowed to more definable
ends—providing services and treatment to enhance the well-being of individuals
(Hamilton, 1956; Perlman, 1949). Under the medical model, social workers essentially study the problems of their clients, diagnose the problems (or strengths, in the
current perspective), and prescribe action steps to produce the desired outcome.
Whether working in child and family services, foster care, mental health, substance
abuse, or gerontology, the social worker today commonly equates practice with
working directly with individual clients to enhance their well-being (Specht &
Courtney, 1994).

The prominence of the medical model remains evident in the NASW Code of
Ethics. The very first sentence of section 1.01 of the code states, "Social workers'
primary responsibility is to promote the well-being of clients" (National Association
of Social Workers, 1999, p. 7). Furthermore, as is evident from the list of ethical
standards in section 1, of the term "clients" is narrowly defined as individuals receiving treatment or services from trained social workers.

While the field's use of psychiatry and Freudian psychology helped to legitimize
social work as a profession, Richmond's and Addams's belief that social workers
could never completely stand in as the social servants of the community was forgotten. On one hand, the profession blossomed during the twentieth century as
social work secured its place as the primary profession in the development and provision of social services (Council on Social Work Education, 2001). On the other
hand, several scholars suggest that social work has tended to focus primarily on

individual needs while neglecting to pay adequate attention to the social and environmental factors that contribute to people's vulnerability, oppression, and poverty. For example, Brueggemann (2002) asserts that current social service organizations (the main employers of social workers) do not promote compassion, empathy, reciprocity, or asset building. Instead, the emphasis on social work licensing and systematic and efficiently run organizations has actually perpetuated social and economic injustice.

McKnight (1995) argues that the growth and professionalization of social work has become dependent upon there being enough people in need of services to validate the need for more social workers. For instance, he states that "We may have reached that point where there are more people in Chicago who derive income from serving the poor than there are poor people" (p. 97). He then raises the question, "Do [social workers] need the welfare clients more than the clients need their service?" (p. 97).

In the same vein, Specht and Courtney (1994) wonder if social work has abandoned its mission altogether. They point out that at a time when social problems have become more difficult and complex, too many social workers are practicing psychotherapy, and too many of them are in private practice. Meanwhile, instead of partnering with volunteers to define and address social problems, social work continues spending too much time and energy staking its claim as the profession that should be called upon to work with an ever-expanding list of populations. As we shall now discuss, there are two reasons why social work is wary of partnering with volunteers.

INSECURITY

Almost a century after the 1915 NCCC annual convention, there are several outward signs that the profession of social work is undeniably secure. Foremost, the job outlook for trained social workers is more optimistic than that for all other human service professions. Social workers are the main providers of social welfare and mental health services in the United States and are represented in growing numbers in other fields, such as substance abuse, aging, schools, health, and employment assistance (U.S. Department of Labor, 2006). Schools of social work have also increased in number. In 2003, there were over 450 BSW programs, almost 160 MSW programs, and 72 social work doctoral programs in North America (Council on Social Work Education, 2003). Moreover, state social work licensure laws and the work of large national membership associations such as the National Association of Social Work and the Council on Social Work Education have earned the publics recognition of social work as a profession. Despite these accomplishments, however, social workers continue to allow Flexner's presentation to raise doubts about our professional standing. As a result, the profession remains preoccupied with its ability to develop discipline-specific knowledge.

Social work simply does not have its own theoretical knowledge base. For example, systems theory emerged from the field of biology; the ecological perspective is derived from anthropology, sociology, and psychology; life course theory is rooted in psychology and sociology; and social exchange theory evolved from psychology, anthropology, and economics (Robbins et al., 1998). Therefore, in this regard, Flexner was and is still correct in his assessment: the fields of professional social work are too numerous and diverse to identify or rely upon a single discipline-specific knowledge base. With this in mind, there are three important questions to consider concerning social work's relationship with volunteers: Should social workers continue searching for discipline-specific knowledge? Does social work need its own theoretical knowledge base to qualify as a profession? And how has social work's relationship with volunteers been affected by the profession's search for its own body of knowledge?

While social work has gained professional status by developing a unified code of ethics, establishing social work licensure and credentials, and implementing an agreed-upon criteria for social work education, it has been unable to develop a specialized body of knowledge. The inability to develop knowledge that is unique to social work is not the result of a lack of effort. In fact, many social workers remain preoccupied with the search. In some cases, social workers have attempted to claim different theories to be primary to social work practice. For example, Robinson (1931) advocated the psychoanalytic contributions to social work practice, Hollis (1970) the psychosocial approach, Smalley (1970) the functional approach, Thomas (1973) behavioral modification, and Saleebey (2002) the strengths perspective. Nevertheless, each theoretical framework is ultimately rooted in knowledge developed by another field. Other social workers have attempted to develop a unique social work knowledge base through scientific research. For example, Thyer (2002) candidly admits having spent his entire career searching for social work's unique knowledge base. After twenty-five years, he has reluctantly come to the conclusion that it is impossible to identify unique social work contributions in any given area of practice research.

The fact that social work cannot claim a unique theoretical knowledge base doesn't necessarily mean social work is not a profession. What it does mean is that the profession must decide how much credence it will continue to give to Flexner's presentation. The time has come for social work to leave Flexner behind. By all other indicators, social work is seen by society as a profession. There is no need for social work to continue evaluating its status other than for self-serving purposes. Yet at various points over the past three decades, major social work journals have published articles and entire issues dedicated to assessing social work's professional status. In each case there is usually some mention of Flexner's influence on the profession and in some cases his presentation is the focal point (see, e.g., Austin, 1983; Goldstein, 1990; Reamer, 1994; Thyer, 2001, 2002).

Flexner (1915) himself questioned his own ability to assess social work. He admitted that his knowledge was too limited, and he doubted his competency in drawing a valid conclusion. Moreover, his six criteria represent only one approach to assessing professional status—an approach based upon a medical model of practice that emphasizes specialization (Austin, 1983; Specht & Courtney, 1994). Social work will never meet this criteria because its focus is the antithesis of specialization. Instead, social work is a profession that applies theories derived from other fields to enhance the well-being of individuals and advocate socially and economically just societies. Social work needs to abandon its preoccupation with identifying a discipline-specific body of knowledge, accept its position as an applied profession, and begin steering all its attention toward interdisciplinary efforts to develop knowledge that will help address specific social problems.

The lack of a unified knowledge base and the preoccupation with finding or claiming one have left social work insecure about its professional status. Gambrill (2001) suggests the profession's insecurity is evident in its reliance on information that is authority based rather than evidence based. As a result, social work remains apprehensive about expanding its relationship with volunteers because it fears it could jeopardize its professional status in society. In the same way, the social work profession has attempted to define itself as separate from its volunteer origins. Partnering with volunteers to deliver services and address social problems gives volunteers access to the social welfare turf that the profession has worked so hard to establish for itself and threatens the profession's perceived authority over that turf. Gambrill (2001) explains that social work has been "bamboozling the public and those who fund service programs into believing that professionals offer unique services that require specialized training and experience" (p. 170). The reality is that social work interventions steeped in psychotherapeutic strategies and a medical-model approach, while serving to protect social work's professional status, are of limited use when it comes to addressing social problems that affect the most vulnerable and oppressed groups of people—the stated emphasis of the work of the profession (National Association of Social Workers, 1999).

Partnering with volunteers is an alternative way for social workers to develop and deliver services. Social workers need to see volunteers as partners in their quest to bring about social change (Bruggemann, 2002). Instead of practicing as experts providing care or as agents representing large social service bureaucracies, social workers can work side by side with volunteers, helping to support and direct them in the promotion of social and economic justice. Expanding practice with volunteers, however, will require social work to gain a level of confidence that will allow it to abandon its obsession with its professional status.

AVOIDANCE

As a result of social work's professional insecurity, the profession has tended to avoid practice with volunteers. A decade after Flexner's presentation, Jane Addams recognized social work's fascination with psychiatry, psychotherapy, and the medical-model approach to practice. While acknowledging their professional benefits, she tried reminding her colleagues of the importance of working with volunteers. Speaking to her colleagues, she posited the following request: "I should like now to ask a favor of the psychiatric social workers. They are the newest and most popular group among us. They are taking great care of the individual who is brought to them, whether he comes as a free nursery child, or whether he comes from the courts. Perhaps we can ask them that they go outside of this individual analysis and give us a little social psychiatric work" (Addams, 1926, p. 7). She then reminded them that, from a clearly ethical point of view, social work must always involve partnering with people in the community who are closest to the poor and are living as best they can.

It appears very few social workers listened to Addams. In fact, a few years later, in a famous address to the 1929 National Conference of Social Work, Porter Lee (1937), director of the New York School of Philanthropy, declared that training volunteers to lead and participate in social movements was no longer a function of social work. Instead, he suggested that social work's primary function was serving individuals through the use of primarily methods based on psychiatric and other psychotherapeutic interventions. His views represented the dominant position in the field. A quick glance at current employment trends indicate that his views are held by the majority of social workers today. Social workers are most likely to work in direct clinical roles that generally do not involve work with volunteers (U.S. Department of Labor, 2006).

The profession as a whole continues to avoid social work practice with volunteers and to ignore both calls for more practice with volunteers and scholarship demonstrating the value of volunteers to the social work profession. Theilen and Poole (1986) have argued that volunteer associations are one of the most effective yet frequently overlooked avenues that social workers have to achieve social change. They suggest that social work educators need to cover content on volunteerism throughout the entire curriculum. Other scholars have suggested that the profession's emphasis on facilitating transactions between the person and the environment makes social workers well suited to educate, support, and partner with volunteers to develop and implement effective services (Anderson & Ambrosino, 1992; Euster, 1984; Forte, 1997; Sherr & Straughan, 2005). Moreover, a few social work scholars, such as Ram Cnaan and Robert Wineburg, have spent their careers teaching students to practice with volunteers. Both have published numerous articles and books imploring the social work community to appreciate the possibilities of working with volunteers. Considering the concerted bipartisan efforts to encourage more volunteerism and localize social welfare services, Wineburg (2001) laments that the social work community has "virtually ignored one of the most important changes to hit local human services systems in many years" (p. 37).

SUMMARY

This chapter took a look at social work's relationship with volunteerism. Despite the origins of the profession in volunteerism, social work has spent the majority of the last ninety years attempting to distinguish itself as a profession that is different from the charitable efforts of people wanting to serve their communities. It is time for social work to stop justifying its own professionalism and begin focusing exclusively on fulfilling its stated mission of "meeting the basic human needs of all people, with particular attention to the needs and empowerment of people who are vulnerable, oppressed, and living in poverty" (National Association of Social Workers, 1999, p. 1).

Currently, social work has the potential to begin a new period in its relationship with volunteers. The landscape of social welfare services has shifted over the past two decades. The responsibility for providing social services is moving away from the federal government into the realm of public, private, and nonprofit organizations at the state and local levels. Along with this shift there has been a concerted effort to encourage volunteers to participate in addressing social concerns. As an important profession in the development, provision, and evaluation of social welfare services, social work's future as an effective and valued profession is significantly related to how successful we are in reclaiming our role as partners to volunteers. If we are to do this, social work must take a fresh look at one of the most important motivations for people to volunteer—religion.

DISCUSSION QUESTIONS AND LEARNING EXERCISES

1. Think of any area of social work practice. Conduct a literature review to examine the early origins of the area of practice you have selected. What role did volunteers play? What role do volunteers currently play? What roles do you think they could play?
2. In 1908 Mary Richmond stated that social workers could never completely stand in as the social servants of the community. Instead, a basic responsibility of social workers was to guide and support the efforts of volunteers. Are Richmond's remarks relevant to social work today? Why or why not?
3. This chapter contends that the social work profession has attempted to separate and distinguish itself from volunteers due to its insecurity about its professional status. Do you agree? Why or why not? If you do not, can you give other reasons to explain the relationship?
4. In 1915 Abraham Flexner's presentation dramatically influenced the direction of the social work profession. In fact, it still continues to influence practice today. How might the social work profession look and operate today had it not given so much weight to his lecture? Describe what you think social work practice will look like in the future. What are the similarities? What are the differences?

6

The Impact of Religion on Social Work's Relationship with Volunteers

RELIGIOUS BELIEFS AND PRACTICES ARE ONE WAY OF CONVEYING SOCIAL values. In addition to empirical knowledge, religious beliefs and practices often foster commitment to a set of norms and behaviors that legitimize a society (Parsons, 1977). In modern societies, religious beliefs and practices commingle with volunteerism in such a significant and complex way that recognizing and appreciating this link is a key for effective social work practice with volunteers.

This chapter examines the interconnection between religion, volunteerism, and social work. After a brief review of the foundations for volunteer service of several world religions, the chapter explores the important sociological function religious groups play in promoting volunteer service, the scope of volunteer contributions made by religious groups, and social work's skittishness with religion and how that has affected the relationship with volunteers.

THE RELIGIOUS FOUNDATIONS OF VOLUNTEER SERVICE

Alan Keith-Lucas (1994), one of the leading scholars in the area of social work and religion, suggests that the desire to help others may have developed as a part of religion. He points out that almost all major religions stress responsibility for all humanity, kindness and justice for the needy, and self-fulfillment through service. Here we discuss how five major world religions emphasize volunteer service.

Judaism and Volunteerism

In Judaism, providing volunteer service is a direct extension of worshiping God. In the first five books of the Bible, known as the Torah, several passages command the Jews to serve one another. For instance, Deuteronomy 10:12, 18–19, states: "And now, O Israel, what does the Lord your God ask of you but to fear the Lord your God, to walk in all his ways, to love him, to serve the Lord your God with all your heart and with all your soul. . . . He defends the cause of the fatherless, and the widow, and loves those who are alien, giving them food and clothing. And you are to love those who are aliens, for you yourselves were aliens in Egypt." It is noteworthy that this passage links service to the Lord with service for those most in need. When Jewish people provide service to others, it represents an outward expression of their love for God. Love for God is thus active and sustained devotion characterized by ongoing commitment to serving others and God. Furthermore, when Jewish people offer support, they are to remember that they are no different from the people receiving help, because they too were once in need of assistance when they were slaves in Egypt.

Later in Deuteronomy 15:7–8, 10–11, Jews learn about the importance of serving the poor. The passage states: "If there is a poor man among your brothers in any of the towns of the land that the Lord your God is giving you, do not be hardhearted or tightfisted toward your poor brother. Rather be openhanded and freely lend him whatever he needs. . . . Give generously to him and do so without a grudging heart; then because of this the Lord your God will bless you in all your work and in everything you put your hand to. There will always be poor in the land. Therefore I command you to be openhanded toward your brothers and toward the poor and needy in your land." Interestingly, in addition to providing services to those in need, both passages indicate the importance of doing so with the right attitude. When a Jew volunteers his or her time and resources, having a gracious attitude is what transforms the service into an act of worship or evidence of devotion to God. The passages do not specify any characteristics of those receiving assistance. Therefore, volunteer service should be extended to everyone who is in need and should not be based upon race, gender, or other distinguishing features.

The Hebrew words *tikkun olam* and *tzedakah* are terms used to communicate the concept of service in Judaism. *Tikkun olam* is generally translated as "healing the world." For many Jews, *tikkun olam* is synonymous with the pursuit of social justice. The word *tzedakah* expresses the ideals of justice and charity according to which people are supposed to provide support without expecting any form of repayment. Maimonides, a rabbi, philosopher, and physician who lived during the Middle Ages, outlined eight levels of *tzedakah,* each of which demonstrates a higher level of virtue:

1. He who gives, but gives grudgingly
2. He who gives less than his share, but does so joyfully
3. He who gives when asked
4. He who gives without being asked
5. He who gives without knowing the receiver, yet the receiver knows the giver's identity
6. He who knows the receiver, but the receiver does not know him
7. Neither party knows the identity of the other
8. He who helps the other before the others suffer need; by loans, or by personal guidance in his affairs, or by setting him up on business or profession, allowing him to earn his own living. (Trepp, 1980)

Thus, the eight levels encourage Jewish people to participate in active and sustained volunteer service, as the highest two levels of *tzedakah* require ongoing service to enhance and maintain the overall well-being of the community.

Christianity and Volunteerism

Christianity is, of course, an outgrowth of Judaism. Jesus himself was a Jew, and many of the ideas of Christianity had their origins in and bear great resemblance to those found in Judaism (Peterson, 1993). In terms of volunteer service, Christianity expands the notion of serving others as worship to serving others as a personal response to the love and compassion displayed in the life and sacrifice of Jesus Christ. In fact, Jesus explains in the book of Matthew that when people serve others it is as if they were serving the Lord himself:

> For I was hungry and you gave me something to eat, I was thirsty and you gave me something to drink, I was a stranger and you invited me in, I needed clothes and you clothed me, I was sick and you looked after me, I was in prison and you came to visit me. Then the righteous will answer him, Lord, when did we see you hungry and feed you, or thirsty and give you something to drink? When did we see you a stranger and invite you in, or needing clothes and clothe you? When did we see you sick or in prison and go to visit you? The King will reply, I tell you the truth, whatever you did for one of the least of these brothers of mine, you did for me. (Matt. 25:35–40)

Then in the book of James, active service is depicted as a vital part of maintaining one's faith and growing as a person who believes in Jesus Christ as the Messiah. According to James, Jesus's brother, having faith is useless if it does not lead to "Loving your neighbor as yourself" (James 2:8), where the word "neighbor" is used to mean members of an entire community, not just the people who live next door. James states, "What good is it, my brothers, if a man claims to have faith but has no deeds? Can such faith save him?" (James 2:14). He later answers his own question by saying, "Faith by itself, if it is not accompanied by action, is dead" (James 2:17).

Finally, in several of his letters, the apostle Paul encourages people to develop their God-given talents and use them to serve the collective good of the community. For instance, he states: "There are different kinds of gifts, but the same spirit. There are different kinds of service, but the same Lord. There are different kinds of working, but the same God works all of them in all men. Now to each one the manifestation of the Spirit is given for the common good" (1 Cor. 12:4–7).

Moreover, Paul insists that the role of church leaders is to help people volunteer. Paul explains that by encouraging people to serve, church leaders help people grow in their relationship with God. He states that the role of pastors and teachers is to "prepare God's people for works of service so that the body of Christ may be built up until we all reach unity in the faith and in the knowledge of the Son of God and become mature, attaining to the whole measure of the fullness of Christ" (Eph. 4:12–13).

Islam and Volunteerism

Islam is based on the teachings of Muhammad. Muhammad was born in 570 CE in Mecca (now Saudi Arabia). At the age of forty, he began having visions, which were revealed to him by the angel Gabriel; these visions lay the foundation for a complete moral and social order that became the tenets of Islam. Volunteerism plays an important part in Islam's moral and social order.

Islam distinguishes between three categories of people based on their faith and commitment. First, there are people who believe that a God exists. Their beliefs, however, are disconnected from how they live out their daily lives. Next, there are people who believe that a God exists, and because of this belief, they feel it is important to follow God's law. Nevertheless, these people often fall short of acting upon God's law. Finally, there are people who make a daily commitment to act upon the realization that God exists. Muslims are people who have submitted to following God's law and make a daily commitment to act upon their beliefs (Edwards, 2001). Volunteerism is therefore conceived as something that should be done by all Muslims, whereby service rendered is evidence of dedication to God.

Similar to the definition set forth in this book, volunteerism in Islam refers to activities that go beyond basic episodic acts of helping. Ahmad Hussein Sakr (2006), who has written extensively on Islam, explains: "We are encouraged to take on a broader role by working to improve the communities we live in; we should be visiting the sick, feeding the hungry, teaching people to read, helping people who have no one to turn to. . . . As Muslims, we see our role as world citizens. The idea of working for a better society or community shouldn't be limited to the Muslim community but should extend to the broader non-Muslim community as well."

Volunteerism is also a part of one of the Five Pillars of Islam. The Five Pillars are religious duties that are considered obligations for all Muslims. The first pillar is the *Shahada,* which is the repeated declaration that there is only one God, Allah, and Muhammad is his prophet, *Shahada* is the most important pillar because it is seen as the basis for all goodness. The other four pillars represent different ways Muslims act upon their faith in Allah—*Salat* is the recitation of prayers five times a day while facing Mecca; *Siyam* is the fasting during Ramadan; *Hajj* is the pilgrimage to Mecca, which Muslims are generally expected to make at least once in their lives; and *Sakat* is giving to and serving those in need. *Sakat* is comprised of two types of giving—obligatory and voluntary. All Muslims pay a tax that is used to spread Islam and care for those in need. At the same time, Muslims are supposed to perform *Sadaga,* which is the voluntary donation of time, money, and other resources to those in need (Stillman, 1975).

Hinduism and Volunteerism

Volunteerism is important in Hinduism as well. Hindus believe in a universal soul with which individuals can be reunited only after they learn to transcend time and space. The highest goal of Hinduism, therefore, is *moksha,* which means redemption or salvation. An individual obtains *moksha* by being released from the wheel of life, which is characterized by an endless cycle of rebirths and all the problems of life. There are three ways of obtaining salvation—the Way of Knowledge, the Way of Devotion, and the Way of Works. The Way of Knowledge (*jnana marga*) involves eliminating mental mistakes and wrongdoing by disciplining oneself to right thinking, which eventually results in the realization that the repeated rebirths weren't necessary. The Way of Devotion involves complete dedication to a god or goddess. Hindus believe that devoting one's entire life to a deity makes it possible to end the cycle of rebirths. Finally, the Way of Works involves releasing oneself from the wheel of life by overcoming the law of karma (the law of deeds). By performing more good deeds than bad, individuals can obtain a higher form of rebirth until they are ultimately released from the wheel of life (Johnson, 1997; Rausch & Voss, 1993).

For Hindus, volunteerism is called *nishkam karma. Nishkam karma* are deeds that are dedicated to serving the good of society without the goal of personal advancement or financial gain. Chapter 11, verse 103, of the Tirukkural (the book of wisdom) emphasizes the importance of *nishkam:* "When help is rendered by weighing the receiver's need and not the donor's reward, its goodness grows greater than the sea." The Rig-Veda, the most important of the sacred Hindu texts, contrasts the importance of volunteer service with the temporary nature of material possessions, "Let the rich man satisfy those who seek help; and let him look upon the long view: For wealth revolves like the wheels of a chariot, coming now to one, now to another" (Rig-Veda 10.117.1–6). Thus, according to the Way of Works, by offering selfless service to society through volunteerism, people can release negative *karma* and achieve salvation (Johnson, 1997; Rausch & Voss, 1993).

Buddhism and Volunteerism

Although there are several forms of Buddhism (i.e., Theravada, Mahayana, Tantric, Zen), each type emphasizes goodwill, benevolence, and compassion for all living things. All Buddhists share a common belief in the four cornerstones that help people achieve nirvana. Nirvana refers to a state of complete and utter peace that one can achieve by seeking moderation and avoiding extremes (Rausch & Voss,1993). The four cornerstones of Buddhism are that (1) people should turn away from extreme religious piety and devotion. Instead, they should concern themselves with practical social issues. (2) People should not spend too much time in philosophical speculation. Instead, they are better off focusing on their inner strengths and achieving practical salvation. (3) This can be achieved through the law of karma and (4) the doctrine of samsara (continual rebirths).

The law of *karma* and the doctrine of samsara are two basic tenets of Hinduism that Buddhists accept in modified form. Whereas Hindus emphasize doing more good deeds than bad in order obtain a higher form of life, Buddhists believe that people can rid themselves of all extreme thoughts and behaviors and experience nirvana in one lifetime. Volunteerism is thought of as one way to avoid extremes and seek moderation (Rausch & Voss, 1993).

Volunteerism is important in Buddhism because it helps people give up *tahna* and focus on living the Eightfold Way. *Tahna* are worldly cravings and desires, such as wealth, lust, and pride, that prevent people from experiencing nirvana by tempting them to seek the wrong things. In contrast, the Eightfold Way is a list of eight elements of "right" living that lead to wholesome thinking and action. Volunteerism is consistent with at least half of the elements—right attitude, right action, right effort, and right mindfulness (Edwards, 2001).

As with any action or behavior, when Buddhists volunteer, they are warned against jumping in and doing too much too soon. Buddhists are advised to follow the middle path of moderation; people providing selfless acts of charity and generosity (called *paramita*) should not be overstretched to the point that they feel hostility, jealousy, boastfulness, or any impure intentions. Otherwise, volunteerism can become another expression of *tahna*. Instead, people are encouraged to take it slowly and gradually expand their efforts (Edwards, 2001).

THE FUNCTIONS RELIGIOUS GROUPS PERFORM IN PROMOTING VOLUNTEERISM

Despite variations in beliefs, rituals, and worship practices, the five religious traditions described above fulfill several underlying sociological functions that promote volunteerism. Religious groups help people channel their commitments, feel connected to others, and become aware of potential social problems that need attention. Let's take a closer look at each function.

Channeling Commitment

Religious groups foster commitment by encouraging people to think about what is truly important. In short, religion guides people to consider the meaning of human existence. Religious groups take up difficult questions, such as what is the purpose of life, what should people care about, and for what things in life should people be willing to die (Ammerman, 2001). As Marty (2000) points out, in the process of addressing such questions, religious leaders invariably cross over to questions about social justice, such as who is responsible for the poor and disenfranchised, to what rights are all humans entitled, and what is the best way of enhancing human well-being and promoting effective social functioning. How people contemplate and derive answers to such questions is often manifested in their actions.

Religion invokes commitment and motivation by cultivating values that encourage people to volunteer. When people have strong religious convictions, those convictions can lead them to take actions to live out those values. Volunteerism, therefore, becomes a direct expression of values that they interpret to be inspired by God (Sherr & Shields, 2005). For example, if people learn from their religious beliefs that it is important to care for the young and for those in crisis, they might volunteer at a youth shelter or crisis center as a way of expressing that value. In the same way, those who believe that people should take care of the environment because God created the environment might volunteer to protect animal rights or to conserve natural resources. As Wald (1987) states, "Human beings will make enormous sacrifices [for good or bad] if they believe themselves to be driven by a divine force" (pp. 29–30).

Feeling Connected

Religion provides a way for people to develop a sense of connectedness. Across religious traditions, after instilling beliefs, a basic function of religion is creating reasons for people to develop relationships. In this regard, religious groups offer one of the few opportunities to bring people together for face-to-face interactions on a regular basis. Over time members of the group develop a sense of community. Ammerman (2001) explains, "They see themselves as family, a community of people who care for each other and do things together" (p. 7). This sense of community, however, is not limited to people within particular religious groups. Religious traditions often cultivate a wider sense of citizenship and participation for individual members and entire groups throughout their communities. Most people who enter political life or work as public servants usually do so out of a sense of religious connectedness with the rest of the community (Marty, 2000). Religious traditions often encourage collective efforts to both introduce people to their beliefs and create a sense of connectedness to the larger community (Wuthnow, 2004).

Volunteerism can be thought of both as an instrument of religious traditions and as an outcome. In both cases, religion and volunteerism interact to build and reinforce social capital. Social capital involves the social networks and ties that are created from interactions that encourage people to care for one another (Coleman, 1988). Putnam (2000) describes two types of social capital that are relevant to the current discussion. Bonding social capital describes networks and ties that help create internal solidarity and trustworthiness. For example, religious groups often use volunteers to teach classes, run committees, host visitors, and help with worship activities. Bridging social capital describes networks and ties that link religious groups to the wider society as when religious groups encourage members to use their knowledge, skills, and energy to participate in activities that can benefit the larger community.

Creating Awareness

Religious groups also function to create awareness of social needs. When religious leaders give sermons, they often address social issues such as poverty, hunger, crime, marriage, child rearing, and alcohol and drug abuse (Wuthnow, 2004). They also encourage certain personal and collective behaviors in response to social issues

(Marty, 2000). For example, some religious traditions insist that people refrain from premarital sex, drinking alcohol, or accumulating excessive wealth. Most religious traditions also strongly encourage people to provide money and other resources in order to care for the poor.

Volunteerism represents another way the religious laity is encouraged to respond to social issues. Although social workers may not always agree with the positions religious leaders take on certain social issues, there is no denying the possibilities when large groups of people are made aware of social issues and encouraged to respond to them. Stated differently, religious groups are one of the few things in society that can bring people together from various social, economic, and political backgrounds; unite them through common beliefs that can transcend their differences; make them aware of social problems; and encourage discussion and action to address those problems.

As social workers looking to partner with volunteers, we should heed Putnam's (2000) words: "Faith communities in which people worship together are arguably the single most important repository of social capital in America" (p. 66).

THE SCOPE OF VOLUNTEER CONTRIBUTIONS MADE BY RELIGIOUS GROUPS

Over the last few decades, a small but growing number of scholars have attempted to calculate the extent of volunteer contributions made by religious groups. Although their attempts have generally yielded inconsistent estimates, one point is clear—religious groups are the source of a very large and active pool of volunteers. For present purposes, let's examine the scope of volunteer contributions from three angles: the number of social service programs offered by religious groups, the number of people who volunteer from religious groups, and the economic impact of their contributions.

The Number of Programs

Religious groups often use volunteers to provide a wide array of different services. In addition to volunteer work related to worship activities, religious congregations use volunteers to run programs such as food pantries, clothing closets, summer day camps, recreational programs for children and adolescents, day care for children and the elderly, soup kitchens for the homeless, health screenings, job counseling, and drug and alcohol prevention programs. Although there is disagreement as to the exact number of programs affiliated with a religion, it appears that 54–93 percent of all religious groups offer at least one of these social service programs.

Many religious groups offer multiple social service programs. Cnaan (2002) suggests that religious congregations throughout the country offer an average of four social service programs. Ammerman (2001) posits that by providing money, space, volunteers, and in-kind donations, religious congregations are actually involved in an average of six community programs. Given that there are between 250,000 and 400,000 religious congregations in the United States, it is reasonable to suggest that these groups provide somewhere between 1 million and 2.4 million service programs nationwide.

Ammerman (2001) divides the programs offered by religious groups into five categories. The most common programs provide direct services, such as emergency food, shelter, and clothing, to people in immediate need. The second most common programs offer education and health services, for example, nursery schools, wellness programs, tutoring programs, after-school programs, Boy Scout troops, and senior centers. Third, though less common, are programs that support community development activities, such as crime watches and neighborhood associations. Many religious groups also sponsor programs through which volunteers provide food, shelter, and medical care for people in third world countries. Finally, some religious groups participate in social policy. For example, religious groups sometimes use volunteers to address broad political concerns ranging from health care and the environment to civil rights.

The Number of People

Members of religious groups are more likely to volunteer than individuals who do not belong to a religious group. More than half of all members of religious groups in the United States volunteer. In contrast, about one-third of the rest of the population volunteers. Although some religious groups refer dozens of people to volunteer with different service organizations, an average of fifteen members from each religious group are involved with three different service organizations. Furthermore, members of religious groups contribute between 147 and 160 hours of volunteer work per month. Over half of those hours are devoted to working with organizations unconnected to their religious groups. Overall, individual members contribute one to four hours of volunteer labor each month in connection to their religious groups (Hodge, Zech, McNamara, & Donahue, 1998; Hodgkinson 1990).

When interpreting the extent of volunteer activity from religious groups, we must keep in mind that these numbers are conservative estimates. Wuthnow (1990) explains that any calculation will generate conservative figures because many religious groups believe that they should not boast about their contributions. Furthermore, he warns against examining volunteerism in religious groups too closely. He believes that because it is so difficult to quantify religiosity or spirituality with any degree of accuracy, the process of collecting rigorous empirical information about volunteerism in religious groups may actually obscure efforts to understand the deepest roots of the connection. Still, of the 61.2 million people who volunteered between September 2005 and September 2006, over a third (35%) volunteered for religious programs (U.S. Department of Labor, 2007). This figure hints at the central role religious groups have in generating and channeling volunteer activity.

The Economic Impact

The economic value of social services provided by religious groups is unclear. In one of the first attempts to measure the fiscal contributions of religious groups, Salamon and Teitelbaum (1984) reported that fewer than 10 percent of religious groups devote as much as $25,000 to the direct provision of community services annually. But subsequent studies suggest much greater amounts. For example, Hodgkinson, Weitzman, and Kirsch (1990) reported that religious groups allocate $19.1 billion to the direct provision of services annually. In their analysis of the 1992 Independent Sector study of religious congregations, Castelli and McCarthy (1998) estimated that congregations spend roughly 20 percent of their budgets on social service programs.

The ambiguity of these figures is the result of the way in which scholars have attempted to define and measure the economic value of such programs. Some studies use formulas that focus on the costs of particular aspects of running social programs (Hodge et al., 1998; Wineburg, 1990). Other studies examine aspects of programs that are more difficult to calculate in terms of monetary value. Hodgkinson (1990) points out that religious groups help build community cohesion, provide informal leadership training, and improve the overall quality of life in a community—contributions to which it is nearly impossible to assign monetary value. Nevertheless, these benefits would be costly to replace.

In an effort to examine the direct and indirect economic contributions of religious groups, the Independent Sector (2007) conceptualizes the value of services in terms of their "replacement value," that is, the cost it would take to replace the services and assistance provided by religious groups. Assessing the value of each volunteer hour to be $18.77 and estimating that volunteers give, on average, four hours per month, the overall economic contribution generated by volunteers is $239 billion each year. Of that total, religiously motivated volunteers contribute $83.7 billion (almost one-third) each year.

SOCIAL WORK'S SKITTISHNESS WITH RELIGION

Until recently, social work has tended to play down religion's impact on the development and delivery of social welfare services. This is ironic given the profession's primary emphasis on ecological and social systems perspectives. When religion is addressed, it is usually done so under the guise of spirituality. Spirituality and religion, however, are not the same. Spirituality is a broad term that refers to the human sense of and search for transcendence and meaning. Canda and Furman (1999) define spirituality as "a universal and fundamental aspect of what it is to be human—to search for a sense of meaning, purpose, and moral framework for relating with self, others, and the ultimate reality" (p. 37). For the most part, social work tends to focus on individual spiritual experiences within the context of direct practice or the spiritual experiences of larger groups as a part of developing cultural competence (e.g., Canda & Furman, 1999; Derezotes, 2005; Hodge, 2003).

Religion, though clearly related to spirituality, is a more specific term. Religion refers to a more formal embodiment of spirituality into relatively specific belief systems, practices, and organizational structures. Canda and Furman (1999) define religion as "an institutionalized pattern of beliefs, behaviors, and experiences, oriented toward spiritual concerns, and shared by a community and transmitted over time in traditions" (p. 37). Social work tends to view organized religious groups in a negative light as institutions whose missions, practices, and views are incongruent with ethical social work practice. The prevalence of this view may explain why minimal attention has been paid to religion's impact on social services in the social work literature.

The small but growing body of literature on this subject that does exist indicates that social workers need to appreciate and pay closer attention to the efforts of organized religion. Wolfer and Sherr (2003) warn practitioners to be cautious about stereotyping organized religious groups. With over two hundred denominations, the American religious world is decentralized in the extreme. Regardless of how social workers view organized religion, there is a growing consensus among social work scholars that the efforts of religious groups to participate in the provision of social services is greater than previously imagined and that there is a great opportunity for social workers to coordinate partnerships with religious groups to deliver effective social service programs. In order to do this, however, workers must be trained to appreciate organized religion and the desire of many religious groups to provide services.

Social work owes much of its existence to organized religion. The last chapter suggested that social work was built upon the efforts of volunteers. In fact, religion is inextricably linked to the volunteerism out of which social work emerged. To discount the central role of religion distorts the history of social work and obscures the ways in which that history might contribute to current practice.

In essence, organized religion is fundamentally connected to the COS movement and the settlement house movement—the beginning of social work. Instead of embracing and appreciating this connection, in their discussion of these movements, mainstream social work textbooks either overlook religion or depict it in a negative light. For instance, COS volunteers are often described in social work textbooks as untrained wealthy women from the church who imposed their beliefs and values on the poor (Morales & Sheafor, 2004; Popple & Leighninger, 2002; Zastrow, 2004). These women, however, were not trying to impose their values. Rather, they were attempting to live out their beliefs by providing assistance to the needy. Moreover, motivated by their religious beliefs, these women hoped to encourage poor families with their own and God's love. As Amato-von Hemert (2002) posits, these volunteers intended their efforts "to reform and uplift the poor, not merely to mitigate their sufferings" (p. 48).

Religion also played a larger role in the settlement house movement than is usually acknowledged by social work textbooks. Although not mentioned in most textbooks, it was Jane Addams's consistent attendance at worship services and Bible studies at Fourth Presbyterian Church that allowed her to recruit volunteers and eventually establish Hull-House. Moreover, England's Toynbee Hall (the model for settlement houses in America) was founded by the Anglican Church in an effort to provide outreach and seek social justice. Crocker (1992) describes the settlement house movement as elaborate partnerships between volunteers, religious groups, and businesses, and Luker (1984) suggests that the settlement house movement is linked to the post–Civil War efforts of churches to offer services for African Americans freed from slavery.

Religious groups can also help social work build and maintain an adequate workforce. As Popple and Leighninger (2004) suggest, people who choose to pursue a career in social work usually do not do so with the goal of making a lot of money. They argue that from their experience, religious beliefs are one of the major reasons people choose social work as a career. They also contend that a steadily increasing number of students share that their religious convictions are a part of why they are considering applying to social work programs. In light of this information, the profession needs to find ways to formally embrace its religiously rooted history and appreciate the impact of organized religion on social welfare today.

RELIGION: THE KEY TO SOCIAL WORK WITH VOLUNTEERS

Acknowledging and appreciating the impact of religion is vital to effective social work with volunteers, perhaps more so than in any other area of practice. And herein lies a major dilemma for the profession. If social workers are going to partner with more volunteers, then they must be ready and willing to partner with religious groups. To do so, the profession will have to reconsider its views of organized religion.

Throughout the 1990s, Democratic and Republican leaders encouraged religious groups and volunteers to accept greater responsibility for providing social welfare services for people in need. For instance, presidents Bill Clinton and George H. W. Bush and First Lady Nancy Reagan crossed party lines to work together to encourage more people to volunteer (Hayslett, 1997). Democratic and Republican leaders officially invited religious groups to provide more services by including Charitable Choice as part of the Personal Responsibility and Work Reconciliation Act of 1996. President George W. Bush has continued to support the participation of religious groups and volunteers. He established the White House Office of Faith-Based and Community Initiatives to work closely with corresponding units in the Departments of Labor, Health and Human Services, Housing and Urban Development, Justice, and Education (Cnaan & Boddie, 2002). Regardless of which party controls Congress following the next election or who is elected the next president, the expanding role of religious groups and volunteers in the provision of social services is likely to continue.

Social Work and Religion Share Similar Values

Social workers interested in fulfilling the profession's primary mission of enhancing human well-being and empowering people who are vulnerable, oppressed, and living in poverty should be optimistic about the expanded involvement of religious groups and volunteers. These groups represent an enormous reservoir of people with resources who, more often than not, share the social work profession's ideals. Of course, there are several hot-topic issues over which some religious groups and some social workers might disagree, such as abortion, assisted suicide, and sexual orientation. However, beneath the blaze of disagreement around such issues, social workers will find that many religious groups embrace the core values of our profession.

Religious groups engage in certain core activities (worship, fellowship, stewardship, and education) that express their mission and values (Ammerman, 2001). A closer look at each will show that social work and many religious groups share more common ground than one might think. In fact, these activities often emphasize or reinforce the core values of social work—service, social justice, valuing the dignity and worth of the person and the importance of human relationships, integrity, and competence (National Association of Social Workers, 1999).

Worship

Providing opportunities for spiritual worship is the first core activity of religious groups. The primary emphasis on worship most readily distinguishes religious groups from social work; however, worship reinforces several core social work values, including service to others, social justice, and valuing the dignity and worth of the person. Like social work, the basic mission of religious groups is to enhance the well-being of people, in this case with an emphasis on the spiritual well-being of people. Worship provides people with an opportunity to reflect on their priorities, recommit to what's really important, and remember that they are not the center of the universe and ought to care for others. Worship also reassures people that they are worthy and have a reason to hope. This is especially true for marginalized and oppressed people (Billingsley, 1999).

Fellowship

The second core activity of religious groups is fellowship. Fellowship is consistent with and reinforces the social work values of integrity and the importance of human relationships. Religious groups work hard to create a community of people who care for one another. In addition to worship, religious groups bring people together for meals, recreation, entertainment, and companionship. Often religious groups also find ways to invite other people in the community to attend or participate in these gatherings. The goal is to create a family-like atmosphere characterized by loyalty, reciprocity, and trustworthiness.

Stewardship

Stewardship is an activity in which religious groups and social work are even more similar. This activity embraces all six of social work's core values. Stewardship involves using the time, talent, and wealth of individuals belonging to religious groups to serve communities. It often focuses on serving the community, advocating social justice, and building relationships. Moreover, many religious groups provide some form of preparation and support before sending laypeople out for either activity. It is important to note that many religious groups see their service to the community as an expression of their beliefs.

Education

Religious groups use educational activities for several purposes. Classroom settings are often used to socialize children and newcomers into religious communities. In addition, many religious groups provide classes to support healthy relationships, make people aware of social injustices, and prepare them to serve the community.

Volunteers Are Often Connected to Religious Groups

Social work practice with volunteers often involves working with a number of people who are somehow connected to religious groups. This is especially the case for social workers attempting to develop community initiatives with volunteers to deliver services together. In such efforts, social workers are likely to network with people who are the most active and committed volunteers in their communities. Although the extent of volunteering may vary by religion and denomination, there is a relationship between active participation in religious groups and volunteering. Moreover, there is evidence suggesting that the direction of the relationship goes both ways. People who are more active in their religious group are more likely to volunteer in their community. At the same time, people who are the most active volunteers tend to be more active in their religious group (Sherr & Shields, 2005). In fact, Greeley (1997) suggests that the high rates of volunteerism in America can be explained by religious motivation. When he controlled for religious participation in his study, he found that the rate of volunteering in America fell significantly. In short, there appears to be no way to avoid religion in considering volunteering. Social work must find a way to acknowledge and appreciate the impact of religious groups by looking for areas of mutual interest in which to develop partnerships while maintaining its stance on issues of disagreement.

DEVOLUTION OR PROGRESS?

Instead of encouraging students and practitioners to acknowledge and appreciate the impact religion has had on the field, many in social work are either skeptical or cynical. The current shift in American social welfare policy to localized services and expanded roles for religious groups and volunteers is commonly referred to in social work as devolution—a term used to elicit fear and caution and to suggest that the current shift is a step backwards to a time when there were no federal social welfare programs and no social services delivered by professionally trained social workers. Perhaps Wineburg (2001) captures social work's derisive stance toward religion best, calling the present period "devilution" (a play on the word "devolution"). He disdainfully asks, "How has conservative thinking and rhetoric, often characterized as right-wing American religion, shaped the design and delivery of social services?" (p. 22). However, when viewed within the context of the historical relationship between volunteerism and social work, it may be more accurate to describe the current era as progressive in its shift from volunteers being primarily responsible for social welfare to volunteers advocating government participation to government and professional social workers becoming primarily responsible to, finally, the current era, where society recognizes the need for an optimal balance of shared responsibility by public, private, professional, nonprofit, and volunteer responsibility for social welfare services (Sherr & Straughan, 2005).

SUMMARY

This chapter examined the impact of religion on social work's relationship with volunteers. Within religious groups, people are made aware of social problems, learn to channel their commitments, and develop a sense of connectedness with others—all important functions that reinforce the ethos needed to support volunteer participation. Although attempts to quantify the volunteer contributions of religious groups have yielded inconsistent estimates, the numbers are too large for social work to ignore. Religious groups probably represent the single largest pool of active and potential volunteers. To access and partner with these volunteers, social work must find a way to acknowledge and appreciate different organized religions. Even though some social workers and some religious groups disagree about certain issues, if social workers approach these groups with the same degree of cultural sensitivity given to other communities, they will find that many religious groups share similar ideals and core values with our profession.

The future relevance of social work as a profession will depend on our ability to move beyond our insecurities and embrace the current era of social welfare. The characterization of the current era as devolution is inaccurate and counterproductive. The expanded role of religious groups and their volunteers is here to stay. In light of the historical relationship between social work, volunteerism, and religion, social workers should view the current era as a step forward as society searches for the right mix of public, private, professional, nonprofit, and volunteer responsibility for social welfare. With this in mind, chapter 7 presents a model to prepare social workers to be leaders in developing effective partnerships with volunteers.

DISCUSSION QUESTIONS AND LEARNING EXERCISES

1. Alan Keith-Lucas suggests that the desire to help others may develop as a part of religion. Do you agree? Why or why not? Can you think of other reasons to explain how people develop the desire to help others?
2. Interview someone you know who has volunteered for at least five years and has done so consistently. Ask him or her to describe some of the reasons behind why he or she volunteers. Ask him or her what, if any, role religion plays in the decision to volunteer.
3. Interview a religious leader. In the interview, share the six core values and ethical principles of social work stated in the Code of Ethics. Ask him or her to what extent the values are consistent with the beliefs and practices of his or her religion.
4. This chapter contends that when considered in historical context, the current era of social welfare is not devolution but progression. Do you agree? Why or why not?

Part III

Reframing the Relationship

7

The Context-Specific Optimal Partnership Model

SOCIAL WORK PRACTICE IS CURRENTLY TAKING PLACE IN THE MOST PRO-gressive era of social welfare in its history. At first the volunteer and private sectors were seen as primarily responsible for providing social welfare services. The role of government, especially the federal government, was minimal. Next, in the process of addressing social problems and attempting to provide services, volunteers advocated that government participation was necessary. Government participation, however, led to a major pendulum shift, where government and professional services became primarily responsible for social welfare while the volunteer and private sectors took on a supplemental role. Currently, the landscape of social welfare services has progressed to the point where society recognizes that the predetermined roles and responsibilities of public, private, professional, nonprofit, and volunteer sectors are not effective in addressing complex social problems. There is a need for an optimal balance of shared responsibility.

This chapter presents the context-specific optimal partnership model (CSOP) as an alternative approach for guiding social work practice with volunteers. Instead of developing services with predetermined roles and expectations, the CSOP model allows the unique circumstances of an issue to determine who is involved and what roles each sector plays in developing policies and programs.

Before we look at the model, it is important to note that the underlying philosophy behind context-specific optimal partnerships is not a completely radical or drastically new approach to social work. In fact, the model is similar to how Jane Addams engaged in social work practice. Remember from chapter 4 that she assessed the unique context of specific social problems, worked with anyone who would help to advance a social cause or activity, and developed credibility with a wide range of people because she cared less about professional identity and more about involving the greatest number of people possible. Finally, she was willing to be a volunteer at times and at other times to partner with volunteers. As Addams recognized over a century ago, partnerships between social workers and volunteers have the power to revitalize the profession's efforts to fight poverty and advocate social and economic justice.

THE MODEL

The CSOP model consists of two main components—assessing the context of the situation and creating optimal partnerships. The components, however, are not what make the model useful. In truth, the components are consistent with the basic generalist social work practices of assessment, intervention, and evaluation. The key difference is in the approach to carrying out the process. The CSOP model calls for social workers to leave behind any preconceived notions about how issues should be defined, who should be involved, or how issues should be addressed when assessing the context. Similar to qualitative research methodology and client-centered therapy, the model encourages social workers to let the answers and the direction of the partnerships emerge in the process of assessing the context and building partnerships. Social workers should maintain a flexible stance that allows them to let the information guide decisions. In some instances, an assessment may lead to partnerships where government and professional services play a primary role in a partnership with volunteers. At other times, an assessment of the context may lead social workers to decide that volunteers will play primary roles, while social workers and other human service professionals fulfill supportive functions.

ASSESSING THE CONTEXT

Assessing the context is a comprehensive process that involves collecting information from multiple sources to understand the organizational, cultural, societal, and social class factors that define the parameters of the context. It involves six interrelated steps. Note that social workers do not necessarily have to follow the steps in the exact order they are presented. The important thing to remember is to gather data from each step and then allow the data to inform the assessment of the specific context. Figure 7.1 shows the assessment process.

Identifying the Social Problem

The first step is identifying a significant social problem. Communities can have a multitude of problems. Social workers need to apply their verbal and nonverbal communication skills to work with a broad spectrum of people in order to understand how communities identify and prioritize issues. Social workers need to remember to distinguish between private troubles and social problems. Private troubles may be tragic and may even warrant the attention of social work services, yet they affect a relatively small group of people, whereas social problems are societal conditions that are perceived to be a threat to a significant proportion of the population. As Ginsberg and Miller-Cribbs (2005) indicate, social problems have the potential to threaten large numbers of people: "Threats may be perceived to exist when the consequences of the problem are costly, when others fear they will be injured because of the problem, or when people believe they might be victims of the problems" (p. 57). Social problems, at least potentially, have solutions.

Figure 7.1 Assessing the context

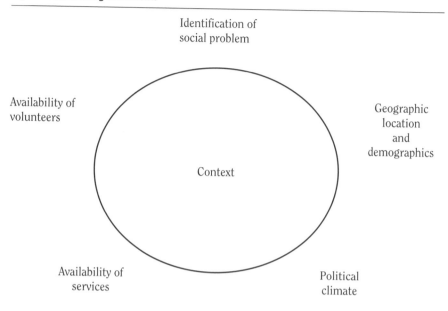

In the process of identifying and prioritizing social problems, it is important for social workers to use their assessment skills to understand how problems emerged. When doing a comprehensive assessment, social workers need to collect information from a variety of sources to determine who identified the problem and how it was brought to the public's attention. For instance, what are people saying in the editorials in local newspapers? What kinds of issues are being discussed at the local diner, at church, and at the grocery market? How are the issues framed by different people? Did the problem begin as a local issue, or is the community facing a social problem that began as a state or national problem and is now affecting local residents? Is the problem isolated to one local community or does it affect surrounding areas?

At times, social workers may disagree with how communities identify and describe their problems. In such instances, it is imperative that social workers exercise restraint and careful judgment in deciding how to proceed. Just as clinicians tune in to all aspects of the verbal and nonverbal communication of clients, social workers must pay attention to all the formal and informal cues and messages they observe. In some cases it may be appropriate for social workers to be educators and raise critical awareness about an issue; however, the CSOP model emphasizes letting clients (in this case the community) assist social workers in defining the problem. Moreover, special attention should be paid to what people from the business community share about a problem. Social workers should avoid discounting views and motives that may at first seem contrary to social work values and ethics. As Jane

Addams realized, social workers, entrepreneurs, and businessmen and women need to work together for any partnership to be effective. Just as she did over a century ago, social workers must be sure to appreciate all charitable impulses and desires, provide business people with direction to channel their charitable desires, and frame the pursuit of social and economic justice in alignment with capitalism.

Understanding the Geographic Location and Demographics

In order to understand the context in which social problems exist, it is often necessary to understand the geographic location and demographics of an area. For instance, communities that are geographically isolated by mountains or bodies of water may have different needs in terms of partnerships than communities with easy access to other areas. In some cases the geographic features are central to the quality of life in a community, and protecting that quality of life is the primary goal.

Although social workers may not be geographic experts, the basic topography of an area can provide valuable information about the social environment. Social workers should answer several questions related to the geographic location of a community. What is the climate? What are the distinctive environmental features (e.g., vegetation, type of soil, elevation, mountains, plateaus, plains, water sources)? Where is the community situated relative to other places? Is a community physically accessible to other communities? Geographic locations of communities can be both unique and similar to other communities. In an assessment, social workers should examine what makes a community unique and what makes it similar to others. As Rubenstein (2002) advises, when assessing geography, social workers must consider "the diversity of culture, economic, and environmental factors, even while making a generalization" (p. 16).

Along with the topography, demographics also provide clues to the context of a community. Given the space, what is the population density? Do people live in one concentrated area or are they spread out? What is the distribution of different age groups, racial and ethnic groups, people of different income levels, and types of housing? Who are the main employers? What are the major religions in the area? Is the community best described as rural, suburban, metropolitan, or urban? Is the population in the community growing, stable, or in decline? When thinking about these questions, social workers should consider not just the area today, but the area as it was a year ago, ten years ago, or even a century ago as well. If there have been major demographic changes, how can they be explained?

Assessing the Political Climate

The political climate has significant influence in shaping communities. Social workers need to spend time and energy assessing the nuances of formal and informal politics if they are to have any chance of developing successful volunteer partnerships. When it comes time to assemble the members of a partnership, it is often a good idea to include elected officials and other community leaders. For starters, find out who the elected officials of a community are. How long have they been in office? Are elected officials local people who have lived in the community for a long time or are they transplants who recently moved to the area? Does one party hold the majority of the elected positions in the community?

Appointed and hired personnel are also important. Who is the city manager? Is there a director of business development or community development? How did these people get their positions? Who is the director of the chamber of commerce? Who is in charge of water, sewer, and sanitation? It is also a good idea to get to know the chief of police and the principals of schools in the area.

In addition to knowing who occupies key positions in communities, it is important for social workers to assess the relationships between the people who hold these positions. Moreover, it is important to have an idea of how communication flows between leaders in the community. How is information shared? Who talks to whom, and who is left out? For instance, does the mayor have a good relationship with members of the school board? Do the members of the city council get along with members of the county government? Are there areas of shared interest around which social workers can bring city and county officials together in collaboration? Finally, how much influence do business leaders and religious leaders have in the community? Which ones have the ear of certain elected and appointed officials?

Assessing the Availability of Services

Communities have different networks of services. The ways in which people look for and receive help can offer social workers clues about a community. Services can be assessed along a continuum from formal to informal assistance. At one end, formal support consists of services provided by agencies and organizations that operate within a bureaucratic structure. Often they are highly impersonal and generally have no prior relationship with the people they serve. Furthermore, they provide care for a limited or specified amount of time and are best suited for tasks that require specialized knowledge or technical skills (Van Tilburg, 1998). Such services may include mental health and substance abuse treatment and services offered by departments of social services, the Veterans Administration, and large nonprofit organizations. Social workers need to know where services in a community are located, who provides what, and how to access these services. In addition, social workers need to assess the disparities that may exist between the needs and preferences of people in a community and the actual services that are available.

Social workers also need to have a keen understanding of the informal supports. Usually family, friends, and neighbors make up informal support networks. Are people connected to friends and family members? When people in communities face crises or hardships, do they have access to informal relationships on which they can rely for support? What types of assistance are informal supports likely to provide? Is there cooperation between formal services and informal supports?

Communities may have other support systems that fall somewhere in between; these are often known as mediating structures. For instance, volunteer service organizations, civic groups, and religious meeting places often provide people with a primary avenue of support outside their families. People often consider such places extensions of their informal support networks; therefore, they are more comfortable asking for and receiving help from these networks than from bureaucratic agencies and organizations. There is even some evidence suggesting that people would be more willing to use formal services if they were provided by these mediating structures (Stuckey, 1997; Tirrito & Spencer-Amado, 2000). It's important for social workers to assess the potential for collaboration with mediating structures as they develop or participate in partnerships with volunteers.

Assessing the Availability of Volunteers

Each community has its own unique collection of volunteers and potential volunteers. Whether you are new to the field or are an experienced practitioner, you should take the time to assess the opportunities people have to volunteer. Start with the usual resources. Check with local colleges or universities to see if they have volunteer coordinators and ask them where they refer students. Find out which volunteer service associations are available (e.g., Rotary, Kiwanis, Lions Club) and how they spend their time and resources. Attend meetings at the local Elks or Masons. In addition, check local newspapers to see the listing of clubs and gatherings. Although these are national associations, each has locally affiliated clubs that are interested in serving their local communities. Make contact with the listed representatives.

Social workers should get to know the religious congregations in the area. Spend time developing rapport with the leaders of churches, synagogues, temples, and mosques. Some communities have interfaith councils where religious leaders from various denominations meet on a regular basis. Such groups tend to offer the largest potential source of volunteers. Social workers need to make it their business to be invited to these meetings.

Most importantly, remember that it doesn't matter whether a group of people gathers to do scrapbooking or build a house with Habitat for Humanity. Whenever there are people gathered in the community, there is an opportunity for what Addams described as social intercourse, which can lead to volunteerism. Finally, look to develop a network of genuine relationships with diverse groups of people and be prepared to use social work skills to bring them together. These all present opportunities for volunteerism.

CREATING OPTIMAL PARTNERSHIPS

Social workers can use their understanding of the specific context of a social problem to form partnerships. Whereas the assessment phase of the model is more fluid, developing optimal partnerships involves a more sequential series of steps.

This is because it takes time and judgment to recruit people, develop a purpose, and maintain active participation over a period of time; this usually takes more time than is required in direct or clinical practice. These steps are:

1. Determine who should be involved.
2. Assess their interests.
3. Develop a primary goal and objectives.
4. Develop strategies and determine the roles of all involved.
5. Implement action plan.
6. Evaluate progress and partnership.

Before we move forward, it is important to note that social workers must never stop assessing the context. As in clinical practice, ongoing assessment is vital to ensuring that partnerships include the right mix of people, remain productive, and know when it is time to terminate. In some cases, conducting community assessments may be a strategy used by partnerships to learn more about a social problem, build cohesion, or recruit more people. Social workers can use their relationship skills to invite others to participate in gathering data about a community. As Kahn (1994) suggests, social workers should always look to invite and include others in the change process. In the process of developing genuine relationships, social workers should teach and model for volunteers how to be critical consumers of information and advocates for their communities.

Determining Who Should Be Involved

Throughout the assessment process, social workers should have one main question in mind—who should be involved in the partnership? Although each situation is unique, a few general guidelines are helpful. First, invite primary stakeholders who represent various interests in the community. At a minimum, try to include people representing the largest employers, hospitals, and the school system, as well as someone with connections to an elected official. It can also be important to include representatives of religious congregations and social service agencies. Also remember to include people of different racial and ethnic backgrounds. If the community is geographically spread out, make sure that there are people invited from every area. This is especially important in rural counties where the majority of the population may be located within the county seat. Unless social workers make a conscious effort to go out and invite people from sparsely populated areas of a county, many people have no way of knowing about the partnership.

Another important group of stakeholders is the people expected to benefit from the efforts of the partnership. Kirst-Ashman and Hull (2006) refer to this group of people as the target system. One of the main premises of this book is that social workers should consider all people in the community, even clients, potential volunteers. Consistent with ethical social work practice, providing the target system

with opportunities to help and participate in the community is the truest embodiment of reciprocal relationships, the principles of self-determination and empowerment, and the strengths perspective. By including representatives of the target
system early in the formation of partnerships, social workers can increase the likelihood that new strategies, programs, and movements will actually be useful. Just
as important from a larger macro systems perspective, including members of target
systems increases the number of people actively engaged in the community—a vital component of a healthy democracy.

During the assessment phase, social workers also should pay attention to people
who appear ambivalent or opposed to efforts to address a certain social problem. In
their process to initiate and implement change, Kirst-Ashman and Hull (2006) discuss the step of neutralizing the opposition. The formative stages of partnerships are
an effective time to prevent or neutralize opposition. Social workers are encouraged
early in the process to identify one or two main figures who represent an opposing
view and invite them to attend a planning meeting and perhaps eventually join the
partnership. Here again, Jane Addams's approach is a good reminder for social workers to validate and appreciate views from segments of the community that may be in
conflict with a social work perspective. Avoid getting into ideological debates.
Instead, use reflective listening and empathetic communication skills to focus on
finding areas in which participants with opposing views hold mutual interests.

Assessing Interests

The goal of the first meeting is to get people interested enough to attend a
follow-up meeting to begin making serious plans to develop a partnership. After a
few moments of getting-acquainted time, the agenda should focus on explaining
why everyone was invited, then assessing their interests. Social workers should
model the use of appropriate self-disclosure to frame what they say about the reason for the meeting. The invitation should already have given participants some
idea of why they were invited to attend. Share enough information to give participants a general sense of the purpose of the meeting, but do not give the details of a
particular view of the problem at hand. Give participants the freedom to share their
views; do not impose ideological judgments up front. Set a pragmatic, collaborative,
and matter-of-fact tone for the partnership.

Next, assess the interests of everyone participating. Ask broad, open-ended
questions that give participants enough latitude to share their opinions. A few useful questions and statements to generate discussion about interests include the following:

◆ "I was wondering if we could take a moment and have everyone share what
it was that interested them in attending this meeting."
◆ "I am interested to know what each of you hopes the result of this meeting
to be."

- "I am assuming that each of you has some awareness about [a particular issue/social problem]. Would each of you please share a little bit about what led you to take the time to attend this meeting?"
- "Let's begin by having each of you share your name, your position, and what agency or constituents you represent." Then as a follow-up question, ask: "If you work for an agency or represent a group of people, could you also share how this meeting might be of interest to them?"

As both facilitators and members of the partnership, social workers should also share their own interests in the issue. It is probably best for the facilitator to share at the beginning. Going first allows social workers to model the parameters of an appropriate response (i.e., how long and how personal the response should be) and to introduce the possibility of collaboration. When sharing, let everyone know that the intention of the meeting is to assess interest in developing a partnership to address a particular social issue. After everyone has had an opportunity to share, use reflective listening and empathetic communication skills to paraphrase a response that highlights areas of mutual interests and concerns. If there is enough "buy in," schedule another meeting with the specific purpose of beginning to plan a partnership. Make sure everyone knows exactly where and when the next meeting will be and how long it will last.

Developing a Primary Goal and Objectives

The next few meetings will focus on developing a primary goal, objectives, and strategies. The primary goal is the vision or end point that the partnership wants to achieve. Normally, the primary goal would already be broadly identified during the process of assessing the context and listening to everyone share their interests. At this point, the group specifies exactly what they want to accomplish. Social workers can use their facilitation skills to lead the group through a process of sharing to generate a statement everyone feels comfortable with. Make sure everyone has an opportunity to share and feels comfortable enough to offer feedback and disagree. Social workers may want to write down what they are hearing as a way for the group to see and reference what is being said. As the group shares, social workers can use their clarifying and interpreting skills to pull together what they hear and begin composing drafts of goal statements. Eventually the group will come to a consensus on one succinct primary goal statement. By summarizing the content and process of the discussion, social workers can make sure everyone knows the primary goal and feels he or she has been a part of developing the goal statement.

The primary goal statement is important because it provides the partnership with its ultimate purpose for working together. However, deciding and stating what the group wants to achieve is different from figuring out how the partnership is going to arrive at its desired outcome. For example, reducing the prevalence of juvenile crimes in Rob County is a worthwhile goal on its own; however, the statement gives no direction as to how the group is going to reduce juvenile crime. That is the purpose of developing objectives. Objectives are specific stepping stones that lead to the achievement of a primary goal. Appropriate objectives for reducing juvenile crime might include developing an after-school program, creating a volunteer mentoring program, and building a skateboarding park and a dirt-bike park to provide recreational activities. Again, the objectives should be developed and agreed upon by the group.

Developing Strategies and Determining the Roles of All Involved

Strategies are behavioral tasks the group must complete in order to achieve the desired objectives, which, in turn, help achieve the primary goal. Groups create strategies by deciding *who* will do *what* by *when: who* is the individual or group of individuals who will accomplish the tasks, *what* is the tasks to complete, and *when* is the time frame for completing the tasks. One important task is figuring out who else needs to be invited to participate in the partnership. Then members can decide who will invite them.

As a group begins listing strategies, there will come a point when everyone realizes that there is a lot of work involved. Thus it is important to work out expectations regarding how time and energy will be spent up front. In order to do this, the group must designate primary, secondary, and supplemental partners. All are equally important to a thriving volunteer partnership; however, each requires different levels of involvement. Primary partners are people who will participate in every aspect of the planning process. They will organize and attend all the meetings, take on the most time-consuming tasks, and keep everyone else informed and feeling connected. Eight to twelve people are usually primary partners. If possible, at least one person should represent the target system, and another person the potential opposition. Secondary partners may not come to every meeting, but they are ready to take on specific tasks. Although they may not come to all meetings, secondary partners are usually kept abreast of what is happening with the partnership. These partners often have special skills or access to resources that the group needs to be successful. Supplemental partners are people who are prepared to participate in isolated events, such as fund-raisers and specific community projects.

Implementing the Action Plan

At some point, the partnership needs to put all its planning into action. On one hand, the group needs to make sure the four previous steps have been completed. On the other hand, it is important for the partnership to do something that gives everyone a sense of achievement. As discussed in chapter 2, people begin and continue volunteering for a variety of reasons, and the reasons can change over time. The feeling that progress is being made can tap into a variety of motivations for different people. Think of getting started as good for achieving the primary goal as well as for developing active and sustained volunteer commitment.

Social workers should think long term. The networking skills used to develop a partnership can set a precedent for how the community addresses other social problems in the future. In other words, build an active and sustained volunteer force that is ready to participate in the community now and in the future. Here are a couple of recommendations for choosing action steps. In the beginning, select initial action steps that have a high probability of being successful and that build toward larger steps to achieve objectives. This way volunteers are likely to experience a sense of participation efficacy. Encourage action steps that require several people to work together to foster group cohesion and integration. When deciding who is going to do what by when, group together people who have certain expertise and skills with people who have an interest in developing those skills. Whatever action steps the group decides to implement, make sure people have enough information and training to feel confident; however, allow for enough flexibility to give volunteers a sense of autonomy as to exactly how they will complete certain tasks.

Evaluating Progress and Partnership

Making evaluation a priority at the beginning of a partnership is a way of providing volunteers with information. Then social workers can use the data gathered to offer feedback to the group. The feedback can be used to maintain focus, provide evidence of time well spent, and adjust how the partnership is operating. In working with volunteers, evaluation serves three major purposes by monitoring processes, outcomes, and volunteer commitment. Evaluations can monitor the processes of the partnership. Process evaluations focus on how the group is getting the work done. Is everyone feeling heard? Are the meetings useful? Is the group staying on task and, at the same time, building rapport? Evaluation can also help determine if the group is making progress toward its primary outcomes. Brun (2005), Ginsberg (2000), and Royce, Padgett, Thyer, and Logan (2005) are all excellent sources to assist social workers in carrying out both types of evaluations.

In the process of developing a context-specific optimal partnership, social workers should pay special attention to monitoring volunteer commitment. Use the volunteer commitment scale to assess how people feel about volunteering for the partnership, how long they have volunteered, how often they volunteer, and how much time they spend volunteering. Galindo-Kuhn and Guzley (2001) have developed a scale to measure volunteer satisfaction. Consider using their scale to make sure people are content with the amount and flow of communication, the opportunities to get together, and the schedule and work assignments. In addition, make sure volunteers feel supported and useful. If people are satisfied and committed, they are likely to recruit other volunteers, to stay around when the group experiences any setbacks or challenges, and to be more interested in helping in the future.

SUMMARY

This chapter set forth the CSOP model as a useful approach to working with volunteers. The model is consistent with basic generalist social work practices of assessment, intervention, and evaluation. The key difference is that the model promotes emergent thinking and action that develops in the absence of any preconceived notions about how issues should be defined, who should be involved, and how issues should be addressed. It is important for social workers to think in terms of cultivating a culture of volunteerism in their communities. Developing volunteer partnerships to address social problems is as much an ongoing philosophy of how to approach social work practice as it is a specific intervention. As White (1997) aptly states, "A golden opportunity may be presenting itself to influence public opinion, and hence public policy, on such issues as welfare reform and crime through the involvement of more [volunteers] who will see and begin to understand what we encounter in our daily work and through our research" (p. 317).

DISCUSSION QUESTIONS AND LEARNING EXERCISES

1. The author contends that the future of social work as a valued profession is related to how willing we are to develop partnerships between secular and sectarian professionals and volunteer, and how successful we are in those endeavors. Do you agree? Why or why not?
2. Think of a social problem in your area and try to answer the following questions. Who first identified the problem? How was it brought to the public's attention? Who is writing editorials about it in the local newspaper? What are they writing? If you were to try to organize a meeting, which of these people would you invite to participate? Are you leaving anyone out? Why?
3. Conduct a geographic assessment of your area. What is the climate? What are the distinctive environmental features of your community? What makes your community unique and similar to other communities? Has the geography or demographics changed over time? How? How might the answers to these questions have an impact on the significant social issues facing your community?
4. Begin expanding your network of potential volunteer partners. Take a look at your local newspaper or Web sites about your community. Look for a listing of community events. Assess how many different civic groups gather each week. Which ones do you think you should know more about in your capacity as a social worker? Contact a couple of them and go to a few meetings.

8

Putting the Context-Specific Optimal Partnership Model into Action

THE PREVIOUS CHAPTER SET FORTH THE CSOP MODEL FOR SOCIAL WORK practice with volunteers. Instead of predetermining the roles of public, private, professional, religious, and volunteer sectors, this model allows the unique circumstances of each issue to determine who is involved and what roles each sector plays in developing policies and programs. In this chapter, three case examples illustrate the model. In two of the cases, the social workers are volunteers who play important roles in developing the partnerships. In the other case, the social worker is hired as a consultant.

The case examples present the context and the steps used to creating optimal partnerships. In review, the assessment areas are:

1. Identification of a social problem
2. Geographic location and demographics
3. Political climate
4. Availability of volunteers
5. Availability of services

The steps to create partnerships are:

1. Determine who should be involved.
2. Assess their interests.
3. Develop a primary goal and objectives.
4. Develop strategies and determine the roles of all involved.
5. Implement the action plan.
6. Evaluate progress and the partnership.

CORAZON DE JESUS

Understanding the Context

West Columbia, South Carolina, is a small city located in the eastern portion of Lexington County within the Columbia metropolitan area. Positioned along the

Congaree and Saluda rivers, West Columbia has long been an independent and self-sustaining city. The city, the majority population of which is white, has experienced a substantial increase in Mexican individuals moving into the area. According to the U.S. Bureau of the Census (1990, 2000), between 1990 and 2000, the number of Mexicans living in West Columbia increased by over 900 percent. Moreover, networks working with Mexican immigrants suggest that the number of Mexicans living in South Carolina is four times higher than the census estimates (Rural Migration News, 2004). As West Columbus is one of the cities with the highest percentages of Mexican residents in South Carolina, it is logical to suppose that the number of Mexicans living in West Columbia is also significantly higher than has been reported by the Census Bureau.

Chartered in 1896 and located in the heart of downtown West Columbia, First Baptist Church of West Columbia was one of the first religious congregations established in the community. The pastoral staff and ministerial laypeople recognized the growing influx of people to the area as well as the effects they were having on their church. On one hand, the increase in the number of Mexican immigrants created the potential for new opportunities for church members to serve those in need and share their beliefs and for the congregation to grow. On the other hand, the pastoral staff and ministerial laypeople recognized that the racist views of a good portion of the congregation and the lack of knowledge of Mexican culture among West Columbia residents were leading long-time members to leave the church. In short, the congregation was at a crossroads in terms of deciding whether to embrace and adapt to the town's new residents and accept the eventual demise of the church or move the church to an area populated by more middle-class and upper middle-class whites. As senior pastor, Lonnie Shull decided that God was calling the church to do the former.

The Context-Specific Partnership

As senior pastor of one of the oldest churches in West Columbia, Lonnie had access to a number of influential people throughout the community, a number of whom were members of the church. First, Charles Abercrombie was a social worker who worked as a field instructor for the College of Social Work at the University of South Carolina as well as an administrator for the Department of Social Services. In the summer of 2002, Charles convinced the dean of the College of Social Work to work with the congregation to develop a faith-based agency to serve Mexican immigrants in West Columbia. The college assisted by placing a bilingual social work student at the church for field placement, supporting a doctoral student in his efforts to serve on a planning committee, and encouraging faculty to serve on the governing board and the advisory board.

Paul Hinson, also a member of the church, served as district governor of the South Carolina Lions Club. In his position as district governor, Paul was interested in figuring out ways to expand the club's local membership by tapping into the growing Mexican population. In fact, before the senior pastor approached him to join the committee that would create Corazon de Jesus, Paul was trying to start a Mexican Lions Club in West Columbia. He became a member of the planning committee and pledged his support as a representative of the South Carolina Lions Club. The Lions Club support consisted of access to hundreds of potential volunteers and potential funding assistance through the International Lions Foundation and fundraising support from local clubs.

Terry Cromer, a layperson at the church, had returned from several mission trips to Spanish-speaking countries with the goal of developing a Mexican ministry at the church. His passion led him to enroll at a local seminary, earn a degree in Christian education, and take on a leadership role in the development of Corazon de Jesus. As one of the elder members and a leader in the church, Terry was instrumental in persuading the congregation to embrace the Mexican ministries.

In addition to the three individuals initially enlisted to establish Corazon de Jesus, over time the partnership expanded to include several other people. The city manager assigned a key member of her staff to participate in the planning. She also guaranteed the support of the police department. The Department of Social Services assigned the regional supervisor and a staff grant writer to the planning committee in the hope that Corazon de Jesus would become a model for faith-based partnerships throughout South Carolina. Finally, Irma Santana and Edgar Medina, administrators of the Hispanic outreach program from the South Carolina Employment Security Commission, served on the planning committee. They helped to ensure that Corazon de Jesus developed programs the local Mexican population would actually use.

Partnership Accomplishments

The partnership's achievements have been significant. In just a few years, the planning committee has formed a strong infrastructure and implemented two programs. The foundation of the infrastructure is the diverse membership of both the governing board and the advisory board. The governing board consists of twelve members, including a member of Congressman Joe Wilson's staff, the former dean of the College of Social Work at the University of South Carolina, the presidents of two historical neighborhood community groups, Pastor Lonnie Shull, the director of Hispanic Missions for the local Southern Baptist Convention office, and several informal leaders from the Hispanic community. The advisory board is made up of small business owners, representatives from local hospitals, pastors from two other churches, professors of social work and public health, and members of the local Lions Clubs.

Prior to the recent influx of Mexican immigrants, this had been a predominantly white community, and residents had had little or no contact with people of different cultural backgrounds. Their distrust of their new neighbors stemmed from their ignorance of Mexican culture and fear of the unknown. Thus, early in the planning stages, Pastor Shull, Charles Abercrombie, Terry Cromer, and the social work intern met with church members on Sunday mornings and Wednesday evening to discuss Mexican culture and talk about the programs they were interested in implementing. The church leaders appealed to the congregation's desire to do their Christian duty and love and help their neighbors. The championing of the programs by the church elders, who were respected throughout the congregation and the community, made people eager to follow their example and become involved with Corazon de Jesus. As they began to attend church functions and socialize with the new members of the community, they came to realize that their prejudices were unfounded, and excitement about the mission of helping their new neighbors became infectious. Due to members' enthusiasm, the church began to host a weekly Spanish-language worship service (which native English speakers also often attend), at which Corazon de Jesus is allowed to keep a portion of the tithes and offerings collected, as well as English-as-a-second-language classes, and Corazon de Jesus now uses the second floor of the church's fellowship hall as office space. At the same time, the services offered by Corazon de Jesus attracted more and more of the community's Mexican and Hispanic residents, and membership, which had previously been dwindling, began to grow. The church hopes that Corazon de Jesus will eventually become a comprehensive ministry providing advocacy and a one-stop location for family services to Mexican immigrants.

A BETTER WAY

Understanding the Context

In 1997, the Robert Wood Johnson Foundation launched a multiyear multimillion-dollar initiative to promote improvements in the care of people nearing the end of life. As part of that initiative, a national study examined the availability and use of end-of-life care in each state. Idaho received one of the lowest grades (D+) for the availability and use of palliative care technology (Last Acts, 2002).

The second component of the initiative was a campaign to promote the development of statewide and local end-of-life coalitions. With financial and educational support from the foundation, the coalitions were created to identify community needs, advocate health-care system changes, and develop projects to support dying people and their families. In 2002, Cheryl Simpson-Whitaker, an MSW and a concerned volunteer, organized representatives of fourteen different organizations to develop A Better Way Coalition, a grassroots movement to improve end-of-life care in Idaho.

The Context-Specific Partnership

Using her networking skills as a social worker, Cheryl assembled a group of stakeholders from several different sectors of the community. The group included several members of the Idaho House of Representatives and the state senate, a representative of the Idaho attorney general's office, the presidents of the Idaho Hospice Association and the Idaho Hospital Association, pastors of several large religious congregations, educators from Boise State University and Northwest Nazarene University, the administrator for the Idaho Commission on Aging, and a volunteer advocate for the Idaho Hispanic community.

Partnership Accomplishments

The partnership's accomplishments were threefold. First, the members of the coalition developed a policy paper that was used to draft and sponsor legislation that will make it easier for Idaho citizens to write advance directives and for them to be acknowledged by health-care facilities throughout the surrounding states in the Pacific Northwest region. Second, A Better Way Coalition has assisted regions throughout Idaho in starting their own coalitions. To date, five local coalitions provide community outreach, public education, and information and referrals about end-of-life care. Even the most desolate rural areas of the state have access to information about pain and symptom management, legal wills, durable power of attorneys, advance directives, patient and family decision making, bereavement services, and religious services.

A Better Way Coalition has also worked with the governor's office, the Idaho chapter of the American Nursing Association, the Idaho chapter of the National Association of Social Workers, and the Idaho Medical Association to offer continuing education on end-of-life issues. One of the major shortcomings of end-of-life care in Idaho is the dearth of medical professionals with palliative care credentials (Last Acts, 2002). At the time of the national study, there were only seventeen people throughout the entire state of Idaho with palliative care certification. A Better Way Coalition has worked to help professionals receive the training necessary for palliative care certification by co-sponsoring the governor's annual conference on aging and providing training at the conference, and by co-sponsoring workshops in different regions throughout the state to ensure that every hospital, hospice, and long-term care facility in the state has at least one person with palliative care certification on staff. The coalition is currently developing end-of-life materials in Spanish and creating a Web site to provide a clearinghouse for information on end-of-life care for all citizens in Idaho.

REDISCOVERING GEM COUNTY

Understanding the Context

Located in Idaho, Gem County is a rural community thirty-five miles long and six miles wide. The city of Emmett, the county seat, sits 2,373 feet above sea level. There are 16,000 people scattered throughout the county, 5,000 of whom live in Emmett. Although close to the state capital, a metropolitan area with over 250,000 people, the county is geographically separated from the city by the foothills of the

Boise Mountains. In other words, despite the short distance, people from Gem County have very little interaction with people from the city—and the majority of them like it that way.

Until recently, the county had two main industries—fruit orchards and logging. When people began settling in the county in the early 1860s, homesteaders found the soil near the Payette River just right for orchard production. At first, only a few acres along the river were planted. Then in 1924 the Black Canyon Dam was built, giving the county one of the best irrigation systems in the nation and the right conditions for massive fruit production (Lyons, 1974).

As settlers continued moving to the county, the demand for housing and the easy access to forestry made logging another booming industry. Eventually Boise Cascade established a mill and became the largest employer in the county. For several decades, millions of board feet of lumber were produced by the mill, which provided jobs for local families and boosted the overall economy.

Then a few years ago, with the influx of foreign produce, most of the orchard farms went out of business. Even worse, due to the influence that environmental groups had on new policies governing logging and grazing, the Boise Cascade Corporation closed the mill. What was once a thriving, independent community was left to look for a new identity.

Like other counties in Idaho, Gem County is required by Title 67 of the 1975 Local Planning Act to develop a comprehensive plan for the area every five years. This comprehensive plan consists of thirteen components relating to the quality of life in the community, ranging from property rights, population, education, and economic development to parks, recreation, and culture.

With the loss of both major industries, Dan Smith, a county commissioner, wanted to put the plan together differently from how it had been done in the past. Common practice for developing the plan was to hire an outside consulting firm to meet with elected officials and write the proposal. However, this time Commissioner Smith wanted to use the planning process to bring the community together. The timing for the planning was just right, as the city of Emmett had just received a proposal from a housing developer to build 1,500 homes up by Black Canyon Dam. The county also expected to receive additional housing proposals as the Boise metropolitan area continued expanding. The new growth could bring renewed prosperity and tax revenue to the county. However, the added growth would literally double the population of the county and forever change the culture from that of a rugged frontier area to a suburbanized bedroom community for transplants commuting to Boise for work each day. The commissioner was not opposed to the growth; he just wanted to make sure that residents had a say in the future of Gem County.

The Context-Specific Partnership

When Dan Smith agreed to take on the responsibility of overseeing the comprehensive plan, he saw it as an opportunity to inject new life into the county. First, he held a meeting with the other county commissioners, the members of the city council, and Marilyn Lopez, the mayor of Emmett. At the meeting, they agreed that the city of Emmett and the county would work together to develop a joint comprehensive plan for the first time in the history of the county. They also agreed to involve as many resident volunteers as possible. The mayor and city council members also decided to enact a 180-day moratorium on new housing construction to give themselves enough time to develop a truly inclusive plan.

Dan Smith then enlisted the help of his friend Fred Weeks to co-chair the planning committee. Weeks was a retired corporate executive with the time to oversee the project and experience working with lots of people. He recommended that the two of them talk with and hire a faculty member from a local university as a consultant to assist with the planning and writing of the comprehensive plan. A week later the two of them met with Brandon Andrews, a professor of social work at the local university.

At the meeting, Commissioner Smith told Dr. Andrews that Don Zillner, a former student, had recommended Dr. Andrews as someone who could help them. Don worked as a social worker in the Emmett office of the Idaho Department of Health and Welfare. He had grown up and lived in Emmett his whole life. His wife was a teacher at the local high school and coached the varsity girl's softball team.

Dr. Andrews was intrigued by the idea of coordinating a large community volunteer effort to write the comprehensive plan. Dan Smith and Fred Weeks were using words like "empowerment," "ownership," and "participation" in the planning process—the kinds of terms that would excite any social worker. So he agreed to work with them as an organizer and a writing consultant.

With Dan Smith's help, Dr. Andrews used his planning and group facilitation skills to organize a meeting in Emmett with all the commissioners, the city council members, the mayor, Fred Weeks, and Don Zillner. Together, the group mapped out a plan. As co-chairs, Dan Smith and Fred Weeks would form a steering committee. The steering committee would consist of thirteen members, each of whom would oversee a group of residents responsible for writing one of the thirteen sections of the comprehensive plan. Next, the groups held several town meetings, placed ads in the local newspaper, and talked to members of different churches to invite as many people as possible to participate. Eventually, the thirteen members of the steering committee formed their own planning groups of twelve to fifteen volunteer members. So there were between 156 and 195 core volunteers who met once a month to work on the plan. In addition, over the course of six months, a number of the groups held town meetings to talk about their particular area. Thus, by the end of the process, there were many more people who had input into the comprehensive plan.

As the steering committee did its work, Dr. Andrews and Don Zillner spent their time conducting an informal study to determine how residents in Gem County would define success for the future of Gem County. Their intent was to develop a vision or mission statement that would help them sort out what fit in the plan. They interviewed a cross-section of residents throughout the county and came to a consensus on several versions of a vision statement. They then brought the potential statements to the steering committee and facilitated a discussion to narrow it down to one statement.

Each group had five months to meet and develop a rough draft of their section of the plan. Next, each of the thirteen members of the steering committee presented and distributed copies of their materials to the rest of the committee. Afterward, Don Smith and Fred Weeks, with the help of Dr. Andrews, merged all the documents, drafted an executive summary, and fine-tuned the final draft. The final plan was then presented to the community in several formats (i.e., hard copies, Internet, highlights in the newspaper, and radio programming).

Partnership Accomplishments

The partnership produced two different kinds of outcomes. From a summative perspective, the partnership developed a comprehensive planning document that could be used to guide the growth of the county. A few of the major highlights included plans to develop a partnership with a local university to begin offering college courses "over the hill" so residents of Gem County could pursue training and education without having to travel to Boise. The plan also called for the go-ahead to be given to the proposed housing development up by Black Canyon, the extra revenue from which would be used to upgrade roads in downtown Emmett and update the water and sewage infrastructure to make the area more attractive to new employers. Apparently the plan is working: two large employers have moved into the area—a sawmill factory that makes wood pallets, and a knife manufacturer that makes knives for hunting, fishing, and domestic uses. Anticipating future housing development proposals, the land usage section of the plan recommended saving a certain number of fifty-acre lots to protect the open rural space valued by the community. Thus future developers are welcome to build new homes; they just have to allow enough access to open lands for all residents.

Perhaps even more important than the summative outcomes, the collective process appears to have injected new life into the community. In a follow-up meeting, Dan Smith and Fred Weeks shared with Dr. Andrews that they were noticing greater turnouts at commissioner meetings. They also noticed that the letters to the editor in the local newspaper were more positive and hopeful. They were looking for other ways to keep the more than 150 volunteers assigned to the different committees active on other community projects. Whereas in most communities throughout the state, comprehensive plans are being developed without residents' knowledge, in Gem County, a recent poll conducted by the local newspaper, indicated that residents felt that the comprehensive plan had become the second most important news story of the year.

COMPARING PARTNERSHIPS

All three of the case examples in this chapter involved context-specific optimal partnerships. In the first example, the social issue took shape within the context of a religious congregation. While the influx of Mexican immigrants probably affected all aspects of community life in West Columbia, it was First Baptist Church that generated efforts to develop the community-wide partnership. The specific context also contributed to the respective roles of and relationships between the religious and secular professionals and the religious and secular volunteers. The church staff and laypeople were the primary members of Corazon de Jesus. The people representing the University of South Carolina and the South Carolina Lions Club were also key partners, but not to the same extent as the church. Corazon de Jesus was housed at the church and received financial and in-kind sustenance from the church. Stated differently, if the congregation had decided not to support the partnership, the Mexican ministry would not exist. Finally, the input from the city manager, the employment security commission, the Department of Social Services, and Congressmen Joe Wilson, while important, were also supplemental. They were valuable to the partnership for specific reasons (i.e., their ability to help promote and advocate for funding, negotiate positive communications with the city government, and create new programs as Corazon de Jesus develops) though not responsible for the primary development and implementation of services.

The second partnership developed as an initiative attempting to improve end-of-life care at the national level. Over time the initiative trickled down from a national study to statewide and then local coalitions. The Robert Wood Johnson Foundation was the primary partner in terms of providing financial resources and infrastructure to help states and local communities develop coalitions. At the state level, a social worker acting as a volunteer was the primary coordinator of the coalition and its activities. All the core members were essential to the coalition's impact with the state legislature, advocacy for possible state appropriations, and networking with regional members to help start local coalitions. However, they operated under the leadership provided by Cheryl Simpson-Whitaker, who operated within the structure of the national initiative. In addition, although professionals from religious congregations participated as members of the statewide and local coalitions, their roles were more supplemental than those of the other organizational entities.

Whereas the first two partnerships were initiated by a pastor and his church and a social worker under the auspices of a national nonprofit foundation, in the example of Gem County, elected officials were primarily responsible for involving volunteers. In addition, the other two partnerships focused on social problems that would take years to address. The partnership in Gem County was organized for a specific time period and task. Though implementing many parts of the comprehensive plan will take further effort, the expectation for participation was limited to the six months needed to develop and write the plan.

Although they developed and operated under completely different circumstances, the three partnerships were similar in that the specific situations determined the makeup of the partnerships as well as each member's roles and responsibilities. In the case of Corazon de Jesus, religious professionals and volunteers played primary roles in developing the partnership. In A Better Way, religious leaders played secondary roles. Guided by the primary oversight and structure of a national philanthropic initiative to improve end-of-life care, volunteers with professional training, the government, and representatives from professional organizations played more substantial roles in the developing coalitions. In Gem County the responsibilities and roles were less distinguishable by religious and secular and professional and volunteer distinctions. Besides the elected officials and the hired consultant, people from various walks of life volunteered as engaged citizens to develop the overall planning document.

SUMMARY

This chapter presented three very different case examples to illustrate the CSOP model. The cases demonstrate the fluidity with which partnerships can develop in light of their unique contexts. Social work practice is occurring in an era and landscape that requires professionals to have a core base of knowledge, values, and skills that are useful in a variety of settings. Most importantly, social workers must learn to be flexible in how they assess social problems and partner with community volunteers. As the primary profession in the development, provision, and evaluation of social welfare services, the utility of social work in the future will have less to do with our efforts to promote professional credibility and more to do with how successful we are in building partnerships with volunteers to deliver services and advocate social and economic justice.

DISCUSSION QUESTIONS AND LEARNING EXERCISES

Practice using the CSOP model for the following two scenarios from chapter 2.

1. You are a social worker who has been hired to work with Ava Harrington at the community mental health center. The center just received a three-year planning grant from the state to develop an educational campaign to inform women about the dangers of using drugs and alcohol during pregnancy. Help Ava develop a context-specific optimal partnership that uses volunteers to carry out the campaign.

2. You are a social worker who works under Duane Wellington at the Department of Social Services. After successfully completing the mission trip to Seattle, Duane decides that a drop-in center in your community would be very helpful to many clients with whom you work at the agency. However, the department doesn't have the funds to develop one on its own. He asks you to figure out a way to get the community involved to help create a drop-in center. Develop a plan to conduct a needs assessment and form a context-specific optimal partnership in which volunteers in the community can help build and run a drop-in center.

3. Identify a social problem or issue in your community and develop a context-specific optimal partnership to address it.

9

Finding Volunteers for Partnerships

SOCIAL WORK PRACTICE WITH VOLUNTEERS BEGINS WITH A SIMPLE NEED—social workers must find volunteers to develop partnerships. But finding volunteers is a process that takes time and effort. It requires the application of basic helping skills, such as building rapport; reflective listening; and expressing warmth, genuineness, and appreciation for others. Just as social workers learn to be conscious and deliberate in how they develop and maintain trusting relationships in clinical practice, they must do the same in strategically developing a diverse network of genuine relationships with people who may become volunteer partners. This chapter will assist social workers in developing a strategic network of genuine relationships that can lead to fruitful volunteer partnerships.

THINK OF BONDING AND BRIDGING CAPITAL

As you interact with friends, family, acquaintances, and colleagues, remember to invest in building both bonding capital (networks and ties that create internal solidarity and trustworthiness) and bridging capital (networks and ties that link people to the wider society). Spend time developing bonding capital by cultivating relationships that foster genuine feelings of belonging, companionship, and mutual respect. Of course, there will always be people with whom we have personality conflicts; for the most part, however, you should make an effort to appreciate and validate others' values, interests, and concerns. At the same time, develop bridging capital by appreciating how each relationship offers the possibility for everyone involved to expand their networks. As social workers with a focus on coordinating and linking people with their environments, we must seek out opportunities to bring people together.

BE STRATEGIC, BUT NOT TOO STRATEGIC

Although developing genuine personal relationships involves using many of the same skills as those used in clinical practice, these relationships are different.

Personal relationships do not have the same external parameters as professional helping situations. The needs and interests of social workers are as important and relevant as the needs and interests of other parties. Personal relationships should be authentic. Social workers should consider expanding their social networks by doing what interests them. If you are interested in cooking, join a cooking club. If you are interested in sports, join a league. If religion is important to you, consider joining a religious congregation, but, most importantly, participate in small group activities where there are opportunities to develop genuine relationships.

CONSIDER JOINING A VOLUNTEER SERVICE ORGANIZATION

While membership in professional organizations is important, it is important for social workers to consider becoming active and committed volunteers in volunteer service organizations. As Theilen and Poole (1986) stated over twenty years ago, volunteer associations are one of the most effective, yet frequently overlooked, avenues that social workers have to achieve social change. They recommend that social workers interested in pursuing social change consider "forming, holding membership in, or collaborating with voluntary associations" (Theilen & Poole, 1986, p. 20).

Volunteer service organizations offer an abundance of resources in terms of money, talents, and interests for developing volunteer partnerships. These organizations are different from large public social service agencies and professional nonprofit organizations in that they are usually structured to give groups or clubs enough autonomy to address the values and concerns of local communities (Brueggemann, 2002). Moreover, these groups are usually attended by a diverse group of people. As members, social workers can help develop relationships, participate as volunteers, and assist in channeling local club efforts to address the most pressing social problems and use their resources most effectively. Just remember to listen to the views and interests of the organization's members and, most importantly, appreciate the value of the group cohesion that these groups nurture by creating opportunities for companionship as well as the benefits of serving their communities.

What follows is a list of fifteen volunteer service organizations that have locally affiliated clubs throughout the United States and other countries. Though not exhaustive, the list provides a good place to start identifying potential groups to join and/or develop partnerships with. These organizations are always looking for new members and new opportunities to collaborate on community service projects. The organizations are usually focused on addressing a few particular social problems; however, the problems are usually defined broadly enough to find reasons to collaborate on most projects.

VOLUNTEER SERVICE ORGANIZATIONS

Organization Name: Altrusa International
Address: 332 S. Michigan Avenue, Suite 1123
                      Chicago, Illinois 60604
Phone: (312) 427-4410
                      (312) 427-8521 Fax
Web Address: www.altrusa.com

Altrusa was started in 1917 by Alfred Durham, a member of Kiwanis who saw the need for a business and professional women's organization. Currently there are 11,350 male and female members in 392 clubs in nineteen countries. Altrusan is a community based grassroots volunteer organization that seeks to address social problems specific to local areas. Volunteers conduct service projects to raise money for local charities, volunteer at battered women's shelters, help runaway teens, build houses for Habitat for Humanity, and do whatever communities need to be better communities.

Organization Name: Benevolent and Protective Order of Elks
Address: 2750 N. Lakeview Avenue
                      Chicago, Illinois 60614-1889
Phone: (773) 775-4700
                      (773) 775-4790
Web Address: www.elks.org

Started in 1868, the Benevolent and Protective Order of Elks is one of the oldest fraternal organizations in the country. There are currently over one million members in more than 2,100 communities. The BPO Elks attempts to promote the ideals of charity, service, and patriotism. Elk members volunteer their time and money for disaster relief, youth programs, drug awareness programs, the promotion of healthy athletic activities, and honoring veterans.

Organization Name: Fraternal Order of Eagles
Address: 1623 Gateway Circle S.
                      Grove City, Ohio 43123
Phone: (614) 883-2200
                      (614) 883-2201 Fax
Web Address: www.foe.com

The Fraternal Order of Eagles was founded in 1898. It has over 1,700 local volunteer clubs throughout the United States and Canada. Over the years, the Eagles have advocated for Workman's Compensation, Mothers and Old Age pensions, and progressive Social Security laws. The main focus of their community service projects is to raise funds for research in areas such as heart disease, kidney disease, diabetes, and cancer. They also raise money to help neglected and abused children and for the elderly.

Organization Name:	The General Federation of Women's Clubs
Address:	1734 N. Street, NW
	Washington, DC, 20036-2990
Phone:	1-800-443-GFWC (4392)
	(202) 835-0246 Fax
Web Address:	www.gfwc.org

In 1890 Jane Cunningham Croly, founder of Sorosis, extended an invitation to women's clubs throughout the country to attend a ratification convention in New York City. Sixty-three clubs attended the convention, where the General Federation of Women's Clubs was formed. The GFWC is the world's oldest women's volunteer service organization. Working locally through thousands of clubs in over twenty countries, GFWC volunteer members support the arts, promote education and civic involvement, and work toward world peace and understanding.

Organization Name:	The Association of Junior Leagues International
Address:	90 William Street, Suite 200
	New York, New York 10038
Phone:	(212) 951-8300
	(212) 481-7196 Fax
Web Address:	www.ajli.org

Formed in 1921, the Association of Junior Leagues International is an organization of women of all races, religions, and national origins who demonstrate an interest in and commitment to volunteerism. There are currently more than 170,000 members in 294 local Junior League clubs in the United States, Canada, Mexico, and the United Kingdom. Junior League community service projects focus on family literacy, historic preservation, building children's museums, women's shelters, school readiness, leadership development, and the specific needs of local communities to make communities healthier.

Organization Name:	Kiwanis International
Address:	3636 Woodview Trace
	Indianapolis, Indiana 46268-3196
Phone:	(317) 875-8755
	(317) 879-0204 Fax
Web Address:	www.kiwanis.org

Founded in 1915, Kiwanis International is a volunteer service organization with more than 280,000 members in 8,400 clubs in ninety-six countries. Kiwanis clubs conduct volunteer community service projects that primarily target children, with a particular emphasis on the special needs of children from prenatal development to age five.

Organization Name:	Knights of Columbus
Address:	1 Columbus Plaza
	New Haven, Connecticut 06510-3326
Phone:	(203) 752-4000
Web Address:	www.kofc.org

The Knights of Columbus is a Catholic men's fraternal benefit society formed in 1881 to offer financial aid, promote civic involvement, and support social welfare for needy families. There are currently 1.7 million members in 12,000 councils throughout the United States, Canada, the Philippines, Mexico, the Dominican Republic, Puerto Rico, Panama, the Bahamas, the Virgin Islands, Guatemala, Guam, and Saipan.

Organization Name:	Lions Clubs International
Address:	Lions Clubs International Headquarters
	300 W. 22nd Street
	Oak Brook, Illinois 605-8842
Phone:	(630) 571-5466
Web Address:	www.lionsclubs.org

Started in 1917, Lions Clubs International is one of the largest volunteer service organizations in the world. There are nearly 1.4 million members in 45,000 clubs in 199 countries and geographic areas. Lions are recognized worldwide for their service to the blind and visually impaired. The Lions are also involved in a variety of other activities to improve their communities, such as programs to improve the environment, provide diabetes awareness, and develop youth programs.

Organization Name:	National Grange of the Patrons of Husbandry
Address:	1616 H Street NW
	Washington, DC, 20006
Phone:	(888) 4-Grange
	(202) 628-3507
	(202) 347-1091 Fax
Web Address:	www.nationalgrange.org

Started in 1867, National Grange is the nation's oldest agricultural organization. Today, there are 300,000 members who volunteer in clubs located in 3,600 local-communities in thirty-seven states. Located mostly in rural areas, Grange volunteers provide service on a wide variety of issues, including economic development, education, family endeavors, and policy legislation designed to ensure a strong and viable rural America.

Organization Name:	The National Exchange Club
Address:	3050 Central Avenue
	Toledo, Ohio 43606-1700
Phone:	(419) 535-3232
	800-XCHANGE (800-924-2643)
	(419) 535-1989
Web Address:	www.nationalexchangeclub.com

This organization was formed in Detroit, Michigan, in 1911. The name "Exchange" was selected to symbolize the exchange of ideas and information on how to better serve communities. Currently, there are 28,000 members in hundreds of volunteer clubs in the United States and Puerto Rico. National Exchange programs focus on four objectives—promoting Americanism; or pride for American symbols; promoting volunteer community service; sponsoring and supporting youth programs; and preventing child abuse while strengthening families.

Organization Name:	Optimist International
Address:	4494 Lindell Boulevard
	St. Louis, Missouri 63108
Phone:	(800) 500-8130
	(314) 371-6000
	(314) 371-6006 Fax
Web Address:	www.optimist.org

Optimist International was formed in 1919, shortly after World War I ended. There are currently 105,000 members who belong to 3,200 volunteer service clubs throughout the United States, Europe, and the Caribbean. Optimist clubs generally focus their community service projects on helping kids. The clubs conduct roughly 65,000 volunteer community service projects each year and raise and spend $78 million in their communities. Since each club is run by members in their local communities, each Optimist group has the flexibility to serve youths in the way that is most effective.

Organization Name:	Rotary International
Address:	One Rotary Center
	1560 Sherman Avenue
	Evanston, Illinois 60201
Phone:	(847) 866-3000
	(847) 328-8554 Fax
Web Address:	www.rotary.org

Rotary was formed in 1905 as a business club that focused exclusively on the professional and social interests of club members. However, its mission soon expanded. Members pool their resources and volunteer their time to serve communities in need. There are currently over 1.2 million members who belong to more than 32,000 clubs in more than 200 countries and geographic areas. Rotary service projects focus on protecting the environment and addressing illiteracy, drug abuse, and the needs of both an aging population and children at risk. Rotary club members also volunteer in cooperative relationships with other organizations, such as Habitat for Humanity.

Organization Name:	Ruritan National
Mailing Address:	Post Office Box 487
	Dublin, Virginia 24084
Physical Address:	5451 Lyons Road
	Dublin, Virginia 24084
Phone:	(540) 674-5431
	(877) 787-8727
	(540) 674-2304 Fax
Web Address:	www.ruritan.org

The first Ruritan club was charted in 1928 as an organization in which community leaders could meet and discuss ways to make their communities better places to live. Unlike other volunteer service organizations, Ruritan rarely has national programs. Instead, the 34,000 members in 1,200 clubs throughout the United States work to meet the needs of their own communities. Volunteer club members usually work with other youth organizations, such as Future Farmers of America, 4-H, and Boy and Girl Scouts. Many clubs also establish and supervise community recreation centers, sponsor little league teams, sponsor anti-litter campaigns, and help those in need.

Organization Name:	Sertoma
Address:	1912 E. Meyer Boulevard
	Kansas City, Missouri 64123
Phone:	(816) 333-8300
	(816) 333-4320 Fax
Web Address:	www.sertoma.org

Established in 1912, Sertoma is an international volunteer service organization with over 20,000 members serving in 650 clubs in Canada, Mexico, the United States, and Puerto Rico. Sertoma's primary service projects are directed toward assisting people with communicative disorders. However, individual clubs identify and do volunteer work on specific needs in different communities.

Organization Name:	Zonta International
Address:	557 West Randolph Street
	Chicago, Illinois 60661
Phone:	(312) 930-5848
	(312) 930-0951 Fax
Web Address:	www.zonta.org

Founded in 1919 in Buffalo, New York, Zonta International is a global volunteer service organization of executives in business and the professions, across political and social boundaries, to advance the status of women worldwide. Zonta currently has over 33,000 members in more than 1,200 clubs in sixty-eight countries and geographic areas. Members offer their time, talents, and money to local and international service programs as well as scholarship and award programs aimed at furthering women's education, leadership, and youth development.

SUMMARY

This chapter offered guidance for finding volunteers for partnership. Finding volunteers involves developing an authentic and strategic network of personal relationships. Social workers are encouraged to put themselves in positions to expand their networks by participating in group activities that are of personal interest to them. They are also encouraged to seriously consider becoming active members of a volunteer service organization in their local communities.

DISCUSSION QUESTIONS AND LEARNING EXERCISES

Spend time looking at the Web sites of some of the volunteer service organizations listed in this chapter. See which ones have a club or chapter in your community. Call or contact someone in your local chapter, and tell him or her you are interested in learning more about their organization. You will likely be invited to attend a meeting and enjoy a meal with members. Go. Enjoy. Observe. Participate.

10

Changing the Context

THE PRECEDING CHAPTERS OFFERED A WAY OF REFRAMING RELATIONSHIPS with volunteers. Chapters 7 and 8 presented the CSOP model as a social work practice method for developing partnerships with volunteers. Chapter 9 demonstrated how social workers can use their communication skills to cultivate relationships with potential volunteers—a key element of sustainable organization and community initiatives relying on volunteer participation.

Recall that the CSOP model consists of two main components—assessing the specific context and creating optimal partnerships. Assessing the context involves collecting information from multiple sources to understand the parameters that define the specific context. The information from the assessment can then be used to develop the optimal mix of professionals and volunteers to address social problems and provide needed services to the community. But what if the assessment shows that the context, at least partially, contributes to the existence of the social problems that need to be addressed? In such cases social workers' interventions must be aimed at adjusting the context.

This chapter focuses on using volunteer partnerships to change the context. Social workers must realize that changing the context requires a long-term perspective. It involves taking a broader view of the social structures that underscore the premises upon which social problems are recognized, defined, and addressed. It also involves creating opportunities for volunteers to participate in shaping social structures and how they respond to social problems. There are two overlapping factors to consider: the impact of social class and the organizational context of most social work practice.

THE IMPACT OF SOCIAL CLASS

Ever wonder who decides what the important beliefs and values of a community are? Who determines the essential needs of a community? Or who decides how the needs of a community are addressed? Taking a broader view of a community's social structures involves understanding the impact of social class. Social class refers to the increased chance that people with common experiences and economic conditions engage in similar thinking and action (Dahrendorf, 1959). Social class affects almost every aspect of functioning in a community (Parsons, 1977). Moreover, cultural norms, values, and behaviors are influenced by the competing interests of people from different social classes; whites, males, and financially privileged individuals have the most influence (Pewewardy, 2007). Let's briefly review the impact of social class on organizations and the social work profession.

Social Class and Organizations

The impact of social class is most apparent in human service organizations. In fact, such organizations can be seen as the meeting space of people from different social classes. Human service organizations develop because enough people recognize the need to address a social problem that affects a significant number of people in a community. Often people in similar social classes (usually white men and women with access to financial resources, professional training, and political power) make decisions regarding the creation of new organizations, how problems are defined, and how services are delivered. At the same time, people needing services (usually those with minimal wealth and less training and access to political power) from organizations are usually not involved in any of the organizations' decision-making processes. Moreover, most human service organizations are staffed by a disproportionate number of white men and women who have more in common with the people making decisions than with the people the organizations wish to help.

Social Class and Social Work

An unspoken reality of social work is that the profession struggles to exist in between the people who are part of the decision-making processes that address social problems and the people for whom such services are intended. Indeed, we want to be equally embraced by people from both worlds. Social workers are in a unique position to bring people from a variety of social class groups together to define and address social problems.

Changing the context involves structurally expanding access to participation in making decisions for human service organizations. However, expanding access first begins with acknowledging that the majority of social workers belong to privileged racial and social classes and cannot step in and represent the needs of vulnerable populations. Instead, social workers need to find ways to include members of vulnerable populations in shaping social policy and the priorities of service. For instance, at some point social workers practicing in departments of social services and community mental health centers will likely recognize that despite different presenting issues, their clients usually share some common characteristics (they are poor, and a disproportionate number belong to minority groups, and they have less access to higher education)—things that can't be addressed by case management, therapy, psychosocial rehabilitation, or medication. Rather, workers need to adjust the context of practice by involving a more diverse group of people in defining the reasons organizations exist and deciding what types of services are needed. As Jane Addams realized, social work practice with volunteers is one way of minimizing the impact of social class and creating structural changes in organizations and communities.

ORGANIZATIONAL CONTEXT OF PRACTICE

For most social workers, providing direct services and advocacy for clients involves more than working within the boundaries of isolated helping relationships. The reality is that most social work practice occurs in an organizational context. The organization defines the scope of practice. Although licensed social workers may feel that they have autonomy when working with clients, the organization ultimately sanctions what can and cannot happen by establishing the mission of the agency and allocating funds to programs and services determined to be within the scope of the mission. Moreover, social organizations, social problems, and services are always intertwined. The services provided by social organizations are responses to the human needs that exist in the community. Dynamic internal and external factors shape the parameters of how organizations define the social problems, how programs function, who receives the services, and who provides the services (Meenaghan, Kilty, & McNutt, 2004). Let's briefly examine two factors that affect organizations.

Leadership of Organizations

The leadership of an organization has great influence over how staff addresses social problems in communities. The leadership is usually responsible for developing mission statements and objectives that outline the reasons for the organization's existence and how it plans to provide services. Leaders have to balance the best interests of clients with those of the agency. If an organization does not have financial resources and the cooperation of the community, it will not survive long enough to provide any services. Some leaders view their roles as facilitating change, whereas others view their roles more as informing staff of the realities of practice. Either way, as much as proposed ideas or services may benefit clients, leaders have a responsibility to think through the impact these ideas or services may have throughout the entire organization. At the same time, if leaders are too cautious, the organization can become irrelevant. Therefore, leaders often approach innovation incrementally and on a small scale. Social workers need to appreciate the survival and maintenance of organizations as legitimate concerns and have the patience needed to change the context. Nevertheless, social workers practicing from a broad perspective must also recognize that due to their more privileged backgrounds, they generally define the nature of social problems and the goals of the organization differently than the vulnerable groups receiving services (Holley & Van-Vleet, 2006; Reisch & Sommerfeld, 2002).

Organizations as Open Systems

Organizations exist in real social space that is influenced by many pragmatic realities, some of which are more visible than others. For instance, most organizations rely on revenue from a variety of sources, including funding from the government and philanthropic foundations. The stipulations established by funding sources can have an impact on how organizations define social problems, assess needs, and provide services. In the same way, organizations often need some type of license or certification to provide services. Whether organizations seek state licensure or accreditation from an outside association, the guidelines for certification affect how agencies will identify needs and deliver services.

In addition, human service organizations are also influenced by other organizations and the community's political climate. Organizations do not provide services in isolation. Rather, organizations exist in a social environment in which they compete and collaborate with other organizations. For instance, clients coping with disabilities may receive services from a mental health center, the Department of Social Services, a group home, an employment security commission, and a vocation rehabilitation center. If a social worker determines that too many clients with disabilities are having difficulty navigating all these different organizations, he may want to advocate for clients to have multidisciplinary teams that develop one treatment plan that all the organizations can use to simplify services. What at first seems like a straightforward and commonsense intervention is actually a complex process that will change the context of practice for every organization that provides services to clients with disabilities. Such an idea is feasible but will require a long-range intervention strategy.

Likewise, gaining an understanding of the political climate can help social workers assess the timing and risk tolerance for changing the context. For instance, if a social worker practicing in a high school wants to develop interventions to address teenage pregnancy, it is important that she assess the extent to which the community recognizes and will tolerate a systemic view as opposed to an individual view of the issue. A community that views teen pregnancy as a problem that exists only because certain adolescents make poor choices and their families are too lenient may be supportive of interventions that target those individuals. However, that same community may not tolerate an education campaign to raise critical awareness of the incidence of teen pregnancy and the lack of after-school programming. If the social worker is too zealous in advocating for the latter, she may bring about negative and unwanted consequences for the school. Assessing the political reality does not mean the social worker should not advocate after-school programming. It does mean that the social worker needs to have a long-range and strategic view of interventions that can create the structural changes required to modify how an organization and community define and address a social problem. Practicing with volunteers is one long-range intervention strategy that social workers can use to work with their organizations to slowly change the context of practice.

STRATEGIES FOR PARTNERING WITH VOLUNTEERS TO CHANGE THE CONTEXT

Working with volunteers to create structural changes involves applying recruitment and retention strategies to modify how people view and interact with people from different social classes. Social workers can partner with volunteers to create structural change by being mindful of who volunteers, the kinds of things volunteers do, and how they perceive their roles while working with organizations and clients. Regardless of the approach used, the underlying task for social workers wishing to change the context is to create opportunities for volunteers to become part of and influence the structure and functioning of social service organizations. Again, though this task appears simple and straightforward, working to create such opportunities is likely to be a long and complex process. However, as social workers apply the strategies below, they can easily identify positive steps that can substantiate their efforts and provide encouragement to continue.

Diversifying the Pool of Volunteers

Because social class has an impact on organizations and the profession, social workers need to be aware of who volunteers. If the people volunteering for an organization identify more with the staff and the administrative leadership than with the organization's clients, they are likely to subscribe to the status quo views of the causes of social issues and the efforts to address them. For instance, if a social worker recruiting volunteers for an organization that provides shelter and crisis intervention for the homeless does such an assessment and finds that the list of volunteers consists entirely of people from affluent, religious, and conservative backgrounds, there is a good chance that the volunteer staff may be ignorant of the causes of homelessness and the kinds of interventions needed to change the context of practice to ameliorate the societal conditions contributing to homelessness.

To begin changing the context, social workers can focus on creating opportunities for clients to become volunteers. Two steps must be taken simultaneously to create such opportunities. First, social workers need to modify how they and their organizations view clients. Applying aspects of social learning theory and systems theory, social workers can adjust the language they and their colleagues use to talk about clients as well as their perceptions of clients. Clients can be more than recipients of services; they can be volunteers, providing relevant insights into social issues. Social workers can adjust their oral and written communication to create new ways to promote reciprocal helping relationships. For instance, as social workers develop treatment or care plans, they can consider developing goals for successful clients to eventually become volunteers, work with clients, and participate in staff meetings and on committees charged with defining how the agency functions. It might also be a good idea to begin setting a precedent of referring to recipients of services as "partners" rather than "clients." As social workers modify the language they use, they can explain why they refuse to use the word "client" and encourage their colleagues to do the same.

While changing how organizations view clients from the inside, social workers also need to use recruiting strategies to encourage people of different backgrounds to volunteer. Remember that recruiting active and committed volunteers begins with creating genuine relationships and bringing people together for any reason. Social workers need to put themselves in positions to develop genuine relationships with people in the communities they are serving. These relationships need to develop slowly, and great care must be taken in developing them. The relationships need to foster mutual trust and interdependence so that potential volunteers see themselves as working *with* social workers and their organizations rather than *for* them.

One way to bring people together is to divide communities into smaller groups and then co-sponsor ongoing social events. For instance, one such community group might consist of families living in a government-subsidized apartment complex. Social workers practicing with families living in the apartment complex (especially volunteer coordinators) can plan and attend public gatherings that give them an opportunity to interact with people who share the same social space and similar concerns for the well-being of their community. In time, social workers can look for opportunities to invite people to partner with them as volunteers to serve their communities and eventually learn how to change the context of practice together.

Shaping How Volunteers Perceive Their Roles

What volunteers do and how they perceive their roles can affect the way they view their participation with social service organizations. Remember from chapter 2 that cultural values can influence why people volunteer and how they see their roles. Although people may begin volunteering in direct service activities and avoid participating in activities that challenge the social order, social workers can change the context of practice by changing how people perceive their roles. Case volunteers see their roles exclusively as meeting the present needs of people needing assistance (tertiary intervention). Whereas case volunteers focus on performing specific tasks for individual cases, volunteers who see themselves as class volunteers focus on ameliorating and preventing the disproportionate risks associated with social problems (secondary and primary interventions) as they relate to shared features of certain groups of people and their environments (Meenaghan et al., 2004).

Helping people make the transition from seeing themselves as case volunteers to viewing themselves as class volunteers involves bringing groups of volunteers together for interaction, support, and education. Remember that these things are important for recruiting and retaining committed volunteers. As volunteers carry out their tasks, social workers can schedule opportunities for small groups of volunteers to discuss their experiences and frustrations with clients. As volunteers share, social workers can use their reflective listening skills to point out similar patterns in their own experiences. Social workers can educate volunteers on some of the issues facing the people they are serving—often issues that aren't being addressed by the organizations and programs in the social environment. Social workers can then ask volunteers to work with them to change the context of practice.

For example, a social worker practicing in nephrology may have case volunteers providing transportation and companionship for people needing dialysis—both important roles in enhancing the well-being of people suffering from end-stage renal disease. As volunteers provide these services, the social worker can organize monthly meetings for volunteers to socialize and support one another. At these meetings, she can facilitate discussions about what volunteers are seeing, thinking, and feeling about their experiences. The social worker can ask probing questions, ask for suggestions, and share her own suggestions. As a result of the discussions, some class volunteers might want to partner with the social worker to create a community garden to make fruits and vegetables more available and affordable. Others may become class volunteers by partnering with the social worker to persuade organizations to address the underlying factors associated with increased risk for end-stage renal disease.

A FINAL WORD

I would like to end the book with the following thoughts: social work is at a crossroads in terms of its role in affecting how underlying social problems are defined and addressed. Up to this point, social work has been the primary profession responsible for providing and evaluating social welfares services. However, as the landscape of social welfare services shifts, social work's future relevance is significantly related to how willing we are to partner with volunteers and how successful we are in doing so.

Social work with volunteers is more than recruiting people to carry out routine direct services or mundane clerical tasks. It is an effective practice method for changing the social environment. Partnerships with volunteers can develop with the purpose of changing the context of practice. By diversifying the pool of volunteers and bringing volunteers together to discuss their experiences, social workers can shape the interactions between people needing and providing help. They also can develop a network of class volunteers who can play a role in the structure and functioning of social service organizations. As Mary Richmond demonstrated a century ago, the central responsibility of the social work profession is to guide and support the effectiveness of volunteers.

References

Addams, J. (1892). *The subjective necessity for social settlements.* Paper presented at the School of Applied Ethics, Plymouth, MA. Jane Addams Papers (reel 46, 552–560), Central Washington University, Ellensburg, WA.

Addams, J. (1897). Growth of the corporate consciousness. *Proceedings of the Illinois Conference of Charities, 40–42.* Jane Addams Papers (reel 46, 795–798), Central Washington University, Ellensburg, WA.

Addams, J. (1898). Significance of organized labor. *International Association of Machinists, Monthly Journal, 10,* 551–552. Jane Addams Papers (reel 46, 868–869), Central Washington University, Ellensburg, WA.

Addams, J. (1899). Trade unions and public policy. *American Journal of Sociology, 4,* 448–462. Jane Addams Papers (reel 46, 902-916), Central Washington University, Ellensburg, WA.

Addams, J. (1910a). Public activities and investigations. *Jane Addams: A centennial reader.* New York: Macmillan.

Addams, J. (1910b). *Twenty years at Hull-House.* New York: Macmillan.

Addams, J. (1910c, January). Why women should vote. *Ladies' Home Journal,* 104–107. Jane Addams Papers (reel 46, 1812–1813), Central Washington University, Ellensburg, WA.

Addams, J. (1911). Recreation as a public function in urban communities. *American Sociological Society, Publications, 6,* 35–39. Jane Addams Papers (reel 47, 92–93), Central Washington University, Ellensburg, WA.

Addams, J. (1917). Address to the Woman's City Club of Chicago. *Meeting of Woman's City Club,* 2–4. Jane Addams Papers (reel 48, 811–813), Central Washington University, Ellensburg, WA.

Addams, J. (1918). The world's food supply and woman's obligation. *General Federation of Women's Clubs Biennial Convention Official Report,* 251–263. Jane Addams Papers (reel 47, 1640–1648), Central Washington University, Ellensburg, WA.

Addams, J. (1922). *Peace and bread in time of war.* New York: Macmillan.

Addams, J. (1926). *How much social work can a community afford? From the ethical point of view.* Jane Addams Papers (reel 48, 719–729), Central Washington University, Ellensburg, WA.

Addams, J. (1930). *The second twenty years at Hull-House.* New York: Macmillan.

Allen, N., & Rushton, J. P. (1983). Personality characteristics of community mental health volunteers. *Journal of Voluntary Action Research, 12,* 36–49.

Amato-von Hemert, K. (2002) Battle between sin and love in social work history. In B. Hugen & T. L. Scales (Eds.), *Christianity and social work: Readings on the integration of Christian faith and social work practice* (2nd ed., pp. 45–58). Botsford. CT: North American Association of Christians in Social Work.

Ammerman, N. T. (2001). *Doing good in American communities: Congregations and service organizations working together.* Hartford, CT: Hartford Seminary, Hartford Institute for Religious Research.

Anderson, J. C., & Moore, L. (1978). The motivation to volunteer. *Journal of Voluntary Action Research, 7,* 51–60.

Anderson, S. C., & Ambrosino, R. N. (1992). Should volunteers be used as direct service givers? In E. Gambrill & R. Pruger (Eds.), *Controversial issues in social work* (pp. 174–175). Boston: Allyn and Bacon.

Astin, A. W., Sax, L. J., & Avalos, J. (1999). Long-term effects of volunteerism during the undergraduate years. *Review of Higher Education, 22,* 187–202.

Austin, D. (1983). The Flexner myth and the history of social work. *Social Service Review, 57,* 357–377.

Bandura, A. (1977). *A social learning theory.* Englewood Cliffs, NJ: Prentice-Hall.

Bandura, A. (1986). *Social foundations of thought and action: A social cognitive theory.* Englewood Cliffs, NJ: Prentice-Hall.

Bandura, A., & Walters, R. H. (1963). *Social learning and personality development.* New York: Holt, Rinehart & Winston.

Barck, O. T., & Lefler, H. T. (1958). *Colonial America.* New York: Macmillan.

Berger, P. L., & Luckman, T. (1967). *The social construction of reality: A treatise in the sociology of knowledge.* Garden City, NY: Anchor Books.

Berger, P. L., & Neuhaus, R. J. (1977). *To empower people: The role of mediating structures in public policy.* Washington, DC: American Enterprise Institute for Public Policy Research.

Billingsley, A. (1999). *Mighty like a river: The black church and social reform.* New York: Oxford University Press.

Billingsley, A., & Caldwell, C. H. (1994). The social relevance of the contemporary church. *National Journal of Sociology, 8,* 1–23.

Black, D., & DiNitto, D. (1994). Volunteers who work with survivors of rape and battering: Motivations, acceptance, satisfaction, length of service, and gender differences. *Journal of Social Service Research, 20*(1/2), 73–97.

Blalock, H. M., Jr. (1989). *Power and conflict.* Newbury Park, CA: Sage.

Blau, P. (1964). *Exchange and power in social life.* New York: John Wiley.

Brayfield, A. H., & Rothe, H. F. (1951). An index of job satisfaction. *Journal of Applied Psychology, 35,* 307–311.

Brueggemann, W. G. (2002). *The practice of macro social work* (2nd ed.). Belmont, CA: Wadsworth.

Brun, C. F. (2005). *A practical guide to social service evaluation.* Chicago: Lyceum Books.

Canda, E. R., & Furman, L. D. (1999). *Spiritual diversity in social work practice: The heart of helping.* New York: Free Press.

Carter, C. F. (1926). *When railroads were new.* New York: Simmons-Boardman.

Castelli, J., & McCarthy, J. D. (1998). *Religion-sponsored social services: The not-so-independent sector.* Retrieved September 18, 2005, from http://members.aol.com/jimcast/aspfn97.htm

Charles, J. A. (1993). *Service clubs in American society.* Urbana: University of Illinois Press.

Clary, E. G., & Orenstein, L. (1991). The amount and effectiveness of help: The relationship of motives and abilities to helping behavior. *Personality and Social Psychology Bulletin, 17,* 58–64.

Clary, E. G., & Snyder, M. (1991). A functional analysis of altruism and prosocial behavior: The case of volunteerism. In M. Clark (Ed.), *Review of personality and social psychology* (pp. 119–148). Newbury Park, CA: Sage.

Clary, E. G., Snyder, M., & Ridge, R. (1992). Volunteers' motivations: A functional strategy for the recruitment, placement, and retention of volunteers. *Nonprofit Management & Leadership, 2,* 333–350.

Clary, E. G., Snyder, M., & Stukas, A. A. (1996). Volunteers' motivations: Findings from a national survey. *Nonprofit and Voluntary Sector Quarterly, 25*(4), 485–585.

Cnaan, R. A. (1999). Our hidden safety net. *Brookings Review, 12*(2), 50–53.

Cnaan, R. A., & Boddie, S. C. (2001). Philadelphia census of congregations and their involvement in social service delivery. *Social Service Review, 75*(4), 559–581.

Cnaan, R. A., & Boddie, S. C. (2002). Charitable choice and faith-based welfare: A call for social work. *Social Work, 47*(3), 224–236.

Cnaan, R. A., & Goldberg-Glen, R. S. (1991). Measuring motivation to volunteer in human services. *Journal of Applied Behavioral Science, 27*(3), 269–284.

Cnaan, R. A., Kasternakis, A., & Wineburg, R. J. (1993). Religious people, religious congregations, and volunteerism in human services: Is there a link? *Nonprofit and Voluntary Sector Quarterly, 22*(1), 33–51.

Coleman, J. (1988). Social capital and the creation of human capital. *American Journal of Sociology, 94,* S95–S120.

Coleman, J. (1994). A rational choice perspective on economic sociology. In N. Smelser & R. Swedborg (Eds.), *The handbook of economic sociology* (pp. 166–180). Princeton, NJ: Princeton University Press.

Council on Social Work Education. (2001). *Educational policy and accreditation standards.* Alexandria, VA: Author.

Council on Social Work Education. (2003). *Directory of colleges and universities with accredited social work degree programs.* Alexandria, VA: Author.

Crocker, R. H. (1992). *Social work and social order: The settlement movement in two industrial cities, 1889–1930.* Urbana: University of Illinois Press.

Cubberly, E. P. (1944). *Public school administration.* New York: Houghton Mifflin.

Curtis, J. E., Grabb, E. G., & Baer, D. E. (1992). Voluntary association membership in fifteen countries: A comparative analysis. *American Sociological Review, 57,*139–152.

Cyr, C., & Dowrick, P. W. (1991). Burnout in crisisline volunteers. *Administration and Policy in Mental Health, 18*(5), 343–354.

Dahrendorf, R. (1959). *Class and class conflict in industrial societies.* Stanford, CA: Stanford University Press.

Danoff, A., & Kopel, S. (1994). What are the motivational needs behind volunteer work? *Journal of Volunteer Administration, 12*(4), 13–18.

Davis, A. F. (2000). *American heroine: The life and legend of Jane Addams.* Chicago: Ivan R. Dee.

Derezotes, D. S. (2005). *Spiritually oriented social work practice.* Boston: Allyn and Bacon.

Dunlop, R. (1965). *Doctors of the American frontier.* New York: Doubleday.

Dye, D., Goodman, M., Roth, M., Bley, N., & Jensen, K. (1973). The older volunteer compared to the nonvolunteer. *Gerontologist, 13*(2), 215–223.

Earle, A. M. (1923). *Home life in colonial days.* New York: Macmillan.

Edwards, L. (2001). *A brief guide to beliefs: Ideas, theologies, mysteries, and movements.* Louisville, KY: Westminster John Knox Press.

Elder, G. (1998). The life course as development theory. *Child Development, 69*(1), 1–12.

Ellis, S. J., & Noyes, K. H. (1990). *By the people: A history of Americans as volunteers.* San Francisco: Jossey-Bass.

Erikson, E. (1963). *Childhood and society* (2nd ed.). New York: Norton.

Euster, G. L. (1984). Volunteerism with the elderly: An innovative interdisciplinary course in graduate education. *Gerontology and Geriatrics Education, 5*(2), 13–23.

Fairlie, J. A. (1920). *Local government in counties, towns, and villages.* New York: Century.

Fan, J. Z., Lackland, D. T., Lipsitz, D. T., Nicholas, J. S., Egan, B. M., Garvey, T. W., et al. (2007). Geographical patterns of end-stage renal disease incidence and risk factors in rural and urban areas of South Carolina. *Health and Place, 13*(1), 179–187.

Fellin, P. (2001). *The community and the social worker* (3rd ed.). Itasca, IL: Peacock.

Field, D., & Johnson, I. (1993). Satisfaction and change: A survey of volunteers in a hospice organization. *Social Science & Medicine, 36*(12), 1625–1633.

Flexner, A. (1915). Is social work a profession? In National Conference of Charities and corrections, *Proceedings of the National Conference of Charities and Corrections at the forty-second annual session held in Baltimore, Maryland, May 12–19, 1915* (pp. 576–590). Chicago: Hildmann.

Forte, J. A. (1997). Calling students to serve the homeless: A project to promote altruism and community service. *Journal of Social Work Education, 33*(1), 151–166.

Freud, S. (1953). Three essays on the theory of sexuality. In J. Strachey (Ed. and Trans.), *The standard edition of the complete psychological works of Sigmund Freud* (Vol. 7, pp. 135–245). London: Hogarth. (Original work published 1905)

Galindo-Kuhn, R., & Guzley, R. M. (2001). The volunteer satisfaction index: Construct definition, measurement, development, and validation. *Journal of Social Service Research, 28*(1), 445–468.

Gambrill, E. (1990). *Critical thinking in clinical practice: Improving the accuracy of judgments and decisions about clients.* San Francisco: Jossey-Bass.

Gambrill, E. (2001). Social work: An authority-based profession. *Research on Social Work Practice, 11,* 166–175.

George, L. (1993). Sociological perspectives on life transitions. *Annual Review of Sociology, 19,* 353–373.

Germain, C. B, & Bloom, M. (1999). *Human behavior in the social environment: An ecological view* (2nd ed.). New York: Columbia University Press.

Gidron, B. (1978). Volunteer work and its rewards. *Volunteer Administration, 11,* 18–32.

Gidron, B. (1983). Sources of job satisfaction among service volunteers. *Journal of Voluntary Action Research, 12,* 20–35.

Gidron, B. (1984). Predictors of retention and turnover among service volunteer workers. *Journal of Social Science Research, 8*(1), 1–16.

Gidron, B. (1985). Predictors of retention and turnover among service volunteer workers. *Journal of Social Science Research, 8*(1), 1–16.

Ginsberg, L. (2000). *Social work evaluation: Principles and methods.* Needham Heights, MA: Allyn and Bacon.

Ginsberg, L., & Miller-Cribbs. (2005). *Understanding social problems, policies, and programs* (4th ed.). Columbia: University of South Carolina Press.

Goldstein, H. (1990). The knowledge base of social work practice: Theory, wisdom, analogue, or art? *Families in Society, 73,* 48–55.

Greeley, A. (1997, May/June). The other civic America: Religion and social capital. *American Prospect,* 68–73.

Hamilton, G. (1956). *Theory and practice in social casework* (2nd ed.). New York: Columbia University Press.

Hareven, T. K. (2000). *Families, history, and social change: Life-course and cross-cultural perspectives.* Boulder, CO: Westview Press.

Hayslett, C. M. (1997, April). Volunteering positively impacts nation's future. *Daily Beacon.* Retrieved June 8, 2006, from http://dailybeacon.utk.edu/issues/v74/n69/vol.69v.html

Herzberg, F., Mausner, B., & Snyderman, B. B. (1959). *The motivation to work.* New York: John Wiley.

Hodge, D. R. (2003). *Spiritual assessment: Handbook for helping professionals.* Botsford, CT: North American Association of Christians in Social Work.

Hodge, D. R., Zech, C., McNamara, P., & Donahue, M. J. (1998). The value of volunteers as resources for congregations. *Journal for the Scientific Study of Religion, 37*(3), 470–480.

Hodgkinson, V. A. (1990). The future of individual giving and volunteering: The inseparable link between religious community and individual generosity (pp. 284–312). In R. Wuthnow, V. A. Hodgkinson, & associates (Eds.), *Faith and philanthropy in America: Exploring the role of religion in America's voluntary sector.* San Francisco: Jossey-Bass.

Hodgkinson, V. A., Weitzman, M. S., & Kirsch, A. D. (1990). From commitment to action: How religious involvement affects giving and volunteering (pp. 93–114). In R. Wuthnow, V. A. Hodgkinson, & associates (Eds.), *Faith and philanthropy in America: Exploring the role of religion in America's voluntary sector.* San Francisco: Jossey-Bass.

Hofstadter, R. (Ed.). (1963). *The Progressive movement, 1900–1915.* Englewood Cliffs, NJ: Prentice-Hall.

Holley, L. C., & vanVleet, R. K. (2006). Racism and classism in the youth justice system. *Journal of Poverty, 10*(1), 45–67.

Hollis, F. (1970). The psychosocial approach to the practice of casework. In R. W. Roberts & R. H. Nee (Eds.), *Theories of social casework* (pp. 33–76). Chicago: University of Chicago Press.

Holmes, T. (1978). Life situations, emotions, and disease. *Psychosomatic Medicine, 19,* 747–754.

Homans, G. C. (1974). *Social behavior: Its elementary forms* (Rev. ed.). New York: Harcourt Brace Jovanovich.

Hudson, P. (1998). The voluntary sector, the state, and citizenship in the United Kingdom. *Social Service Review, 72*(4), 452–465.

Husserl, E. (1970). *The crisis of European sciences and transcendental phenomenology.* Evanston, IL: Northwestern University Press.

Hutchinson, E. D. (2003). *Dimensions of human behavior: Person and environment* (2nd ed.). Thousand Oaks, CA: Sage.

Independent Sector. (2007). *Value of volunteer time.* Retrieved August 31, 2007, from http://www.independentsector.org/programs/research/volunteer_time.html

Jarrett, M. (1919). The psychiatric thread running through all social case work. *Proceedings of the National Conference of Social Work* (pp. 587–592). New York: Russell Sage Foundation.

Jenner, J. R. (1982). Participation, leadership, and the role of volunteering among selected women volunteers. *Journal of Voluntary Action Research, 11,* 27–38.

Johnson, J. (1997). *The path of the masters.* Punjab, India: Radha Soami Satsang Beas.

Kahn, S. (1994). *How people get power* (Rev. ed.). Washington, DC: NASW Press.

Kanter, R. M. (1972). *Commitment and community: Communes and utopias in sociological perspective.* Cambridge, MA: Harvard University Press.

Katz, D. (1960). The functional approach to the study of attitudes. *Public Opinion Quarterly, 24,* 163–204.

Katz, M. B. (1996). *In the shadow of the poorhouse: A social history of welfare in America.* New York: Basic Books.

Keith-Lucas, A. (1994). *Giving and taking help* (Rev. ed.). Botsford CT: North American Association of Christians in Social Work.

Kenworthy, M. (1929). Psychoanalytic concepts in mental hygiene. *Family, 7,* 213–223.

Kirst-Ashman, K. K., & Hull, G. H. (2006). *Generalist practice with organizations and communities* (3rd ed.). Belmont, CA: Wadsworth.

Laidler, H. W. (1968). *Boycotts and the labor struggle.* New York: Russell & Russell.

Last Acts. (2002). *Means to a better end: A report on dying in American today.* Washington, DC: Author.

Lawler, E. E. (1973). *Motivation in work organizations.* Monterey, CA: Brooks/Cole.

Lee, J. (1994). *The empowerment approach to social work practice.* New York: Columbia University Press.

Lee, P. R. (1937). *Social work cause and function and other papers.* New York: Columbia University Press.

Livingstone, E. A. (Ed.). (1997). *The Oxford dictionary of the Christian Church* (3rd ed.). New York: Oxford University Press.

Luker, R. E. (1984). Missions, institutional churches, and settlement houses: The black experience, 1885–1910. *Journal of Negro History, 69,* 101–113.

Lynde, E. D. (1924). The place of psychiatry in a general case work agency. *Proceedings of the National Conference of Social Work* (pp. 438–441). Chicago: University of Chicago Press.

Lyons, R. B. (1974). *The village that grew.* Boise, ID: Lithocraft.

Maddi, S. R. (1996). *Personality theories: A comparative analysis* (6th ed.). Pacific Grove, CA: Brooks/Cole.

Marshall, T. H. (1964). *Class, citizenship, and social development.* New York: Doubleday.

Marty, M. E. (2000). *Politics, religion, and the common good: Advancing a distinctly American Conversation about religion's role in our shared life.* San Francisco: Jossey-Bass.

Marx, K., & Engels, F. (1955). *The communist manifesto.* New York: Appleton-Century-Crofts. (Original work published 1848)

Maslow, A. H. (1968). *Toward a psychology of being* (2nd ed.). New York: D. Van Nostrand.

Maslow, A. H. (1970). *Religions, values, and peak experiences.* New York: Viking.

McKnight, J. (1995). *The careless society: Community and its counterfeits.* New York: Basic Books.

McLean, S. L., Shultz, D. A., & Steger, M. B. (2002). *Social capital: Critical perspectives on community and "Bowling Alone."* New York: New York University Press.

Meenaghan, T. M., Kilty, K. M., & McNutt, J. G. (2004). *Social policy analysis and practice.* Chicago: Lyceum Books.

Miller, L. E., Powell, G. N., & Seltzer, J. (1990). Determinants of turnover among volunteers. *Human Relations, 43,* 901–917.

Morales, A. T., & Sheafor, B. W. (2004). *Social work: A profession of many faces* (10th ed.). Boston: Allyn and Bacon.

Morrow-Howell, N., Kinnevy, S., & Mann, M. (1999). The perceived benefits of participating in volunteer and educational activities. *Journal of Gerontological Social Work, 32*(2), 65–80.

Morrow-Howell, N., & Mui, A. (1989). Elderly volunteers: Reasons for initiating and terminating service. *Journal of Gerontological Social Work, 13*(3/4), 21–34.

National Association of Social Workers. (1999). *Code of ethics of the National Association of Social Workers.* Washington, DC: Author.

Naylor, H. (1967). *Volunteers today: Finding, training, and working with them.* New York: Association Press.

O'Neill, J. V. (2002). Paraprofessionals: Answer to shortage? *NASW News, 47*(6), 3.

Ozminkowski, R. J., Supiano, K. P., & Cambell, R. (1991). Volunteers in nursing home enrichment: A survey to evaluate training and satisfaction. *Activities, Adaptation, & Aging, 15*(3), 13–43.

Paolicchi, P. (1995). Narratives of volunteering. *Journal of Moral Education, 24,* 159–173.

Paradis, L. F., & Usui, W. M. (1989). Hospice staff and volunteers: Issues for management. *Journal of Psychosocial Oncology, 7,* 121–140.

Parker, S. R. (1992). Volunteering as serious leisure. *Journal of Applied Recreation Research, 17,* 1–11.

Parsons, T. (1977). *The evolution of societies.* Englewood Cliffs, NJ: Prentice-Hall.

Pearce, J. L. (1983). Job attitude and motivation differences between volunteers and employees from comparable organizations. *Journal of Applied Psychology, 68,* 646–652.

Penner, L. A. (2000). Promoting prosocial actions: The importance of culture and values. *Journal of Social Philosophy, 31*(4), 477–487.

Penner, L. A., & Finkelstein, M. A. (1998). Dispositional and structural determinants of volunteerism. *Journal of Personality and Social Psychology, 74,* 525–537.

Perlman, H. H. (1949). Generic aspects of specific casework settings. *Social Service Review, 23*(2), 293–301.

Peterson, R. D. (1993). *A concise history of Christianity.* Belmont, CA: Wadsworth.

Pewewardy, N. (2007). *Challenging white privilege: Critical discourse for social work education.* Alexandria, VA: CSWE Press.

Popple, P. R., & Leighninger, L. (2004). *Social work, social welfare, and American society* (6th ed.). Boston: Allyn and Bacon.

Pumphrey, R. E., & Pumphrey, M. W. (Eds.). (1961). *The heritage of American social work.* New York: Columbia University Press.

Putnam, M. C. (1887). Friendly visiting. *Proceedings of the 14th Annual Conference of Charities and Corrections* (pp. 255–260). Boston: A. Williams.

Putnam, R. D. (2000). *Bowling alone: The collapse and revival of American community.* New York: Touchstone.

Rappaport, J. (1987). Terms of empowerment/exemplars of prevention: Toward a theory for community psychology. *American Journal of Community Psychology, 15*(2), 121–148.

Rausch, D. A., & Voss, C. H. (1993). *World religions: Our quest for meaning.* Valley Forge, PA: Trinity Press.

Reamer, F. G. (1994). The evolution of social work knowledge. In F. G. Reamer (Ed.), *The foundations of social work knowledge* (pp. 1–12). New York: Columbia University Press.

Reisch, M., & Sommerfeld, D. (2002). Race, welfare, reform, and nonprofit organizations. *Journal of Sociology and Social Welfare, 29*(1), 155–177.

Richmond, M. E. (1908). *The good neighbor in the modern city.* Philadelphia, PA: Lippincott.

Rietschlin, J. (1998). Voluntary association membership and psychological distress. *Journal of Health and Social Behavior, 39,* 348–355.

Rines, E. F. (1936). *Old historic churches of America.* New York: Macmillan.

Robb, C. C. (1931). Changing goals of psychiatric social work. *News-Letter, 1,* 1–2.

Robbins, S. P., Chatterjee, P., & Canda, E. R. (1998). *Contemporary human behavior theory: A critical perspective for social work.* Needham Heights, MA: Allyn and Bacon.

Robinson, V. (1930). *A changing psychology in social work.* Chapel Hill: University of North Carolina Press.

Robinson, V. (1931). Psychoanalytic contributions to social case work treatment. *Proceedings of the National Conference of Social Work* (pp. 329–346). Chicago: University of Chicago Press.

Rothman, J., Erlich, J. L., & Tropman, J. E. (2001). *Strategies of community intervention* (6th ed.). Itasca, IL: Peacock.

Royce, D., Padgett, D. K., Thyer, B. A., & Logan, T. K. (2005). *Program evaluation: An introduction* (Rev. ed.). Belmont, CA: Wadsworth.

Rubenstein, J. M. (2002). *The cultural landscape: An introduction to human geography* (7th ed.). Upper Saddle River, NJ: Prentice-Hall.

Rural Migration News. (2004, July). *Midwest, Southeast.* Retrieved July 9, 2004, from http://migration.ucdavis.edu/rmn/more.php?id=835_0_2_0

Sakr, A. H. (2006). Volunteerism in Islam. *Young Muslims: In pursuit of Allah's pleasure.* Retrieved May 3, 2006, from http://yougmuslims.ca/articles/display.asp?ID=62

Salamon, L. M., & Anheier, H. K. (1996). *The emerging nonprofit sector: An overview.* Manchester: Manchester University Press.

Salamon, L. M., & Teitelbaum, F. (1984, September/October). Religious congregations as social service agencies: How extensive are they? *Foundation News, 62–65.*

Saleebey, D. (2002). *The strengths perspective in social work.* Boston: Allyn and Bacon.

Scheier, I. H. (1980). *Exploring volunteer space.* Washington, DC: Volunteer.

Schutz, A. (1967). *The phenomenology of the social world.* (G. Walsh & F. Lennert, Trans.). Evanston, IL: Northwestern University Press.

Schwartz, F. S. (1977). The professional staff and the direct service volunteer: Issues and problems. *Journal of Jewish Communal Service, 54*(2), 147–154.

Setterson, R. A., & Mayer, L. U. (1997). The measurement of age, age structuring, and the life course. *Annual Review of Sociology, 23,*233–161.

Sherr, M. E. (2003a). Infusing volunteerism into the HBSE curriculum of MSW programs. *Aretê, 27*(1), 81–87.

Sherr, M. E. (2003b). *Social work and volunteerism: Exploring factors that influence volunteer commitment.* Unpublished doctoral dissertation, University of South Carolina, Columbia.

Sherr, M. E., & Shields, G. (2005). Exploring the influence of religion among the most active volunteer service club members. *Social Work and Christianity, 32*(2), 133–150.

Sherr, M. E., & Straughan, H. H. (2005). Social work, volunteerism, and the church: An historical overview and look into the future. *Social Work and Christianity, 32*(2), 97–115.

Sibicky, M. (1992). *Motivations underlying volunteerism: Differences and similarities between student and senior citizen volunteers.* Paper presented at the annual meeting of the Southeastern Psychological Association.

Sider, R. J., Olson, P. N., & Unruh, H. R. (2002). *Churches that make a difference: Reaching your community with good news and good works.* Grand Rapids, MI: Baker Books.

Sills, D. L. (1957). *The volunteer: Means and ends in a national organization.* Glencoe, IL: Free Press.

Smalley, R. (1970). The functional approach to casework practice. In R. W. Roberts & R. H. Nee (Eds.), *Theories of social casework* (pp. 77–128). Chicago: University of Chicago Press.

Smith, D. H. (1981). Altruism, volunteers, and volunteerism. *Journal of Voluntary Action Research, 10,* 21–36.

Smith, J. Z. (Ed.). (1995). *The HarperCollins dictionary of religion.* San Francisco: HarperCollins.

Smith, M. B., Bruner, J., & White, R. (1956). *Opinions and personality.* New York: John Wiley.

Smith, P. C., Kendall, L. M., & Hulin, C. L. (1969). *The measurement of satisfaction in work and retirement.* Chicago: Rand McNally.

Spacapan, S., & Oskamp, S. (Eds.). (1992). *Helping and being helped.* London: Sage.

Specht, H., & Courtney, M. E. (1994). *Unfaithful angels: How social work has abandoned its mission.* New York: Free Press.

Stebbins, R. A. (1996). Volunteering: Serious leisure perspective. *Nonprofit and Voluntary Sector Quarterly, 25*(2), 211–224.

Stevens, E. S. (1991). Toward satisfaction and retention of senior volunteers. *Journal of Gerontological Social Work, 16*(3/4), 33–41.

Stillman, N. A. (1975). Charity and social services in medieval Islam. *Societas: A Review of Social History,* 5, 105–116.

Stuckey, J. C. (1997). A community of friends: The Sunday school class as a conduit for social contacts and social support among older women. *Journal of Religious Gerontology, 10*(3), 53–71.

Stukas, A. A., Snyder, M., & Clary, E. G. (1999). The effects of mandatory volunteerism on intentions to volunteer. *Psychological Science, 10*(1), 59–64.

Taylor, C. (1989). *Sources of the self.* Cambridge, MA: Harvard University Press.

Theilen, G. L., & Poole, D. L. (1986). Educating leadership for affecting community change through voluntary associations. *Journal of Social Work Education, 22*(2), 19–29.

Thibaut, J. W., & Kelley, H. H. (1959). *The social psychology of groups.* New York: John Wiley.

Thomas, E. (1973). Behavioral modification and casework. In R. W. Roberts & R. H. Nee (Eds.), *Theories of social casework* (pp. 181–218). Chicago: University of Chicago Press.

Thompson, A. M. (1995). Latent cosmopolitan and local orientation among rural emergency service volunteers. *Nonprofit and Voluntary Sector Quarterly, 24*(2), 103–115.

Thyer, B. A. (2001). What is the role of theory in research on social work practice? *Journal of Social Work Education, 37*(1), 9–25.

Thyer, B. A. (2002). Developing discipline-specific knowledge for social work: Is it possible? *Journal of Social Work Education, 38*(1), 101–113.

Tirrito, T., & Spencer-Amado, J. (2000). Older adults' willingness to use social services in places of worship. *Journal of Religious Gerontology, 11*(2), 29–42.

Tocqueville, A. de. (1966). *Democracy in America.* (J. P. Mayer & M. Lerner, Eds.). New York: Harper and Row. (Original work published 1835)

Trattner, W. I. (1999). *From poor law to welfare state: A history of social welfare in America.* New York: Free Press.

Trepp, L. (1980). *The complete book of Jewish observance.* New York: Summit Books.

Turner, J. H. (1986). *The structure of sociological theory* (4th ed.). Chicago: Dorsey.

U.S. Bureau of the Census. (1990). *Census 1990 summary file.* Retrieved July 9, 2004, from http://factfinder.census.gov/servlet/DTTable?_bm=y&-context=dt&-ds_name=Dec_1990_

U.S. Bureau of the Census. (2000). *Census 2000 summary file.* Retrieved July 9, 2004, from http://factfinder.census.gov/servlet/DTTable?_bm=y&-context=dt&-ds_name=DEC_2000_

U.S. Department of Labor. (2005). *Volunteering in the United States, 2005.* Retrieved December 23, 2005, from http://www.bls.gov/news.release/volun.nr0htm

U.S. Department of Labor. (2006). *Occupational outlook handbook.* Retrieved March 27, 2006, from http://www.bls.gov./oco/ocos060htm

U.S. Department of Labor. (2007). *Volunteering in the United States, 2006.* Retrieved August 22, 2007, from ftp://ftp.bls.gov/pub/news.release/volun.txt

Van Tilburg, T. (1998). Losing and gaining in old age: Changes in personal network size and social support in a four-year longitudinal study. *Journal of Gerontology: Social Sciences, 53B,* S313–S323.

Vroom, V. H. (1964). *Work and motivation.* New York: John Wiley.

Wald, K. D. (1987). *Religion and politics in the United States.* New York: St. Martin's Press.

Wharton, C. S. (1991). Why can't we be friends? Expectations versus experiences in the volunteer role. *Journal of Contemporary Ethnography, 20*(1), 79–106.

White, B. (1997). The summit place for America's future: A place for social work? *Social Work, 42* (4), 317–318.

Wiehe, V. R., & Isenhour, L. (1977). Motivation of volunteers. *Journal of Social Welfare, 4*(2/3), 73–79.

Wilson, J., & Janoski, T. (1995). The contribution of religion to volunteer work. *Sociology of Religion, 5*(2), 137–152.

Wilson, J., & Musick, M. (1997). Who cares? Toward an integrated theory of volunteer work. *American Sociological Review, 62,* 694–713.

Wineburg, B. (1990). Volunteers in service to their community: Congregational commitment to helping the needy. *Journal of Volunteer Administration, 9*(1), 35–47.

Wineburg, B. (1994). A longitudinal case study of religious congregations in local human services. *Nonprofit and Voluntary Sector Quarterly, 23*(2), 159–169.

Wineburg, B. (2001). *A limited partnership: The politics of religion, welfare, and social welfare.* New York: Columbia Press.

Wolfer, T. A., & Sherr, M. E. (2003). American congregations and their social programs. In T. Tirrito & T. Casio (Eds.), *Religious organizations in community services: A social work perspective* (pp. 23–50). New York: Springer.

Wuthnow, R. (1990). *Improving our understanding of religion and giving: Key issues for research.* San Francisco: Jossey-Bass.

Wuthnow, R. (2004). *Saving America? Faith-based services and the future of civil society.* Princeton, NJ: Princeton University Press.

Zastrow, C. (2004). *Introduction to social work and social welfare: Empowering people* (8th ed.). Pacific Grove, CA: Brooks/Cole.

Index

Page numbers followed by *t* refer to tables.